STUDENT UNIT GUIDE

NEW EDITION

AQA A2 Government & Politics Unit 3A

The Politics of the USA

Colleen Harris

Series Editor: Eric Magee

Philip Allan Updates, an imprint of Hodder Education, an Hachette UK company, Market Place, Deddington, Oxfordshire OX15 OSE

Orders
Bookpoint Ltd, 130 Milton Park, Abingdon, Oxfordshire OX14 4SB
tel: 01235 827827
fax: 01235 400401
e-mail: education@bookpoint.co.uk
Lines are open 9.00 a.m.–5.00 p.m., Monday to Saturday, with a 24-hour message answering service. You can also order through the Philip Allan Updates website: www.philipallan.co.uk

ISBN 978-1-4441-6191-5

First printed 2012
Impression number 5 4 3 2
Year 2016 2015 2014 2013

Cover photo: C/Fotolia

Typeset by Integra, India

Printed in Dubai

Hachette UK's policy is to use papers that are natural, renewable and recyclable products and made from wood grown in sustainable forests. The logging and manufacturing processes are expected to conform to the environmental regulations of the country of origin.

Contents

Getting the most from this book 4

About this book 5

Content Guidance

The electoral process and direct democracy 9

What is a caucus? • What is a primary? • How important are the national nominating conventions? • What are the key features of the presidential campaign? • How important are the media in election campaigns? • Campaign finance • What is the Electoral College and how does it work? • The use of direct democracy in the USA • What are recall elections? • Some comparative features of UK electoral processes

Political parties 23

How do the parties differ? • Internal coalitions • Party organisation • Party decline and party renewal • The two-party system in the USA • Comparison with UK parties

Voting behaviour 33

Partisan alignment • Parties and their core voters • What social and economic factors influence voter choice? • Partisan de-alignment • Abstention in US elections • Some comparisons with the UK

Pressure groups 41

What is a pressure group? • What are the main types of pressure group in the USA? • Why has activity grown in recent years? • How do they achieve their aims? • Access points in the political system • What are the most important factors affecting the success of pressure groups? • What 'outsider' strategies are pursued by US pressure groups? • Are pressure groups a threat to democracy? • Are there checks to pressure group power? • Political action committees • Comparisons with UK pressure groups

Questions & Answers

Introduction 48

Question 1 Electoral process and direct democracy 51

Question 2 Political parties 57

Question 3 Voting behaviour 64

Question 4 Pressure groups 69

Knowledge check answers 75

Index 79

Getting the most from this book

Examiner tips

Advice from the examiner on key points in the text to help you learn and recall unit content, avoid pitfalls, and polish your exam technique in order to boost your grade.

Knowledge check

Rapid-fire questions throughout the Content Guidance section to check your understanding.

Knowledge check answers

1 Turn to the back of the book for the Knowledge check answers.

Summary

Summaries

● Each core topic is rounded off by a bullet-list summary for quick-check reference of what you need to know.

Questions & Answers

Exam-style questions

Examiner comments on the questions

Tips on what you need to do to gain full marks, indicated by the icon **e**.

Sample student answers

Practise the questions, then look at the student answers that follow each question.

Examiner commentary on sample student answers

Find out how many marks each answer would be awarded in the exam and then read the examiner comments (preceded by the icon **e**) following each student answer. Annotations that link back to points made in the student answers show exactly how and where marks are gained or lost.

About this book

This guide has been written to help students opting for AQA Unit 3A, The Politics of the USA, to prepare more effectively. Its aim is to provide students with a clear outline of the way in which the unit is structured and examined, as well as a summary of the content for each part of the unit. Unit 4A, The Government of the USA, is covered in a separate unit guide.

How to use this guide

The Content Guidance section looks at the core content of the unit, focusing on the four areas covered in the specification, including key concepts and theories. The greater focus at A2 on analysis and evaluation is stressed, as well as the need for the effective use of evidence and examples to back up arguments.

The Questions and Answers section covers assessment objectives and levels of response at A2, and advice on achieving examination success. Student responses to examination questions at A2 are included, explaining why students gain, or fail to gain, higher-level marks for their responses and how examination responses could be improved to achieve higher marks and grades.

Although no previous knowledge of US government is required in this unit, it may be useful to you to have some outline knowledge of the way in which US government is structured especially through the constitution, to aid contextual awareness and general understanding of the unit. Similarly, it will be beneficial at the beginning of the course for you to have some basic knowledge of the USA itself, such as key events in its history, its size and socioeconomic, ethnic, religious and regional diversity, its changing demographics and its dominant values, to provide a useful context for understanding its politics.

Specification at a glance

The AQA Unit 3A specification below shows in more detail the key concepts associated with each of the four parts of the unit. It also provides helpful amplification of the core content of the unit as a guide for studying, revision and exam practice.

The electoral process and direct democracy

Key concepts	Content and amplification
• Open, closed and 'invisible' primaries • The caucus system • Balanced ticket • Candidate and issue-centred campaigns • Momentum • Soft and hard money • Negative campaigning • Insider and outsider candidates • Fixed terms • Swing states	• The main characteristics of presidential and congressional elections and the main influences on their outcomes • Candidate selection and nomination through the primary and caucus system and the role of the national nominating conventions • Debates concerning the workings and outcomes of the Electoral College and its impact on campaigns

Key concepts	Content and amplification
	• The significance of money as a factor in electoral success and the impact of the media on campaigns and candidates • Direct democracy at state level through the use of referendums, initiatives, propositions and recall elections, and debates concerning their use • Comparisons with the UK electoral process to illustrate arguments

Political parties

Key concepts	Content and amplification
• Liberalism • Conservatism • Big tent parties • Internal coalitions • Neo-liberal and neo-conservative • New right • Religious right • Compassionate conservatism	• The two main political parties and their differing ideologies, values, policies and traditions • The factionalised nature of the parties: the reasons for, and consequences of, their internal divisions • Party organisation • Recent changes to the parties and reasons for these changes • Debates over party decline or renewal • Debates concerning the weakness of US parties • Reasons for two-party dominance and the significance of third parties and independent candidates • Comparisons with UK parties to illustrate arguments

Voting behaviour

Key concepts	Content and amplification
• Partisanship • Alignment and de-alignment • Gender gap • New Deal coalition • Democratic overload • Differential abstention • Ticket splitting • Swing voters	• Consideration of the main variables affecting the way people vote in the USA and their relative importance • The long-term determinants of American electoral behaviour including socioeconomic status, gender, age, race and ethnicity, region and religion • The significance of partisan alignment and de-alignment • Links between the parties and their core voting coalitions • Recency factors in voting behaviour including different issues and candidates at different elections and their relative importance • Factors causing change in voting behaviour • The causes and consequences of split-ticket voting and high levels of abstention • Comparisons with UK voting behaviour to illustrate arguments

Pressure groups

Key concepts	Content and amplification
• Pluralism • Elitism • Lobbying • Access points • Single-issue groups • Corporate power • Direct action • Iron triangles • Clientelism	• The meaning of political pluralism and debates about its extent in the USA • Types and classification of pressure groups, including economic, moral, environmental, ethnic, gender and issue-based groups • Sectional and cause groups • Debates concerning the methods and tactics used by pressure groups to influence decision making and the reasons for success or lack of it • The relative power of pressure groups vis-à-vis political parties • Controversies over the extent of pressure groups' power in the USA • The role and significance of political action committees, especially regarding electoral finance • Comparisons with UK pressure groups to illustrate arguments

How to do well in Unit 3A

It is important to recognise that A2 units are more demanding than AS units. After a year of studying politics, however, the groundwork has been covered, so that the greater A2 challenges can be faced with confidence.

Make sure that you are very familiar with the unit 3A specification, including:

- the four areas of the unit content on which questions will be based
- the number of questions on the paper and the marks for each section
- the choice of questions and the type of questions
- the assessment objectives and the levels of response

You can get a copy of the AQA specification through the website www.aqa.org.uk. This includes sample questions, mark schemes and the generic assessment criteria, which should guide your studies.

Read

From day 1, be prepared to read widely around the subject to broaden and deepen your knowledge of American politics and American political issues. Reading should include:

- UK and US quality newspapers and websites and their coverage of American politics as it happens. Using these resources can be particularly rewarding in terms of picking up contemporary evidence and examples and also in reinforcing and extending a general interest in and engagement with the subject matter of the unit
- up-to-date textbooks on American politics

- articles in *Politics Review* that are focused on specific topics, which should be used to reinforce your class notes
- current affairs journals such as *Time* or *Newsweek* and *The Economist* (which includes an excellent American Survey section) which have extensive coverage of American political issues that should stimulate as well as inform
- A. J. Bennett's *US Government and Politics Annual Update*, published by Philip Allan Updates

Watch

Watch the television news regularly, paying special attention to American political stories as they happen, to update your notes.

Note

Use notebooks to record significant American political developments and issues, otherwise some key changes and events that take place while you are studying and are not in your textbooks will be forgotten. These notes can be a very effective supplement to your textbook and class notes.

File

Try to keep an organised file from the beginning, filing your notes in an order that makes sense to you and can be understood by you. It is then possible to summarise these notes on index cards during your intensive revision programme at the end.

Review

It is important to review your notes on a regular basis — this means you are learning as you go along, avoiding last-minute panics. Revision means revisiting, but this should be revisiting specification topics that you already know, not trying to learn them from scratch for the examinations. Last-minute panic revision of topics not fully understood should always be avoided, as it is rarely successful.

Reduce your notes to manageable proportions

It helps to rewrite or reformat your notes and you can transfer all the key points that need to be known onto revision index cards, with one card for each part of a topic. This will make learning much more manageable.

Study and revise all four areas of the unit

Remember, there are no predictable questions in examinations, and if you study and revise selectively, leaving large gaps in your overall knowledge and understanding of American politics, it could be disastrous for your result. Work to understand all four areas of the unit as laid out in the specification and to see any important links between them.

Content Guidance

This section of the guide aims to address the key areas of content in the four sections of the AQA Unit 3A specification: Elections and direct democracy, Political parties, Voting behaviour and Pressure groups. It focuses on the main theories, issues and debates in these four areas and explains the key concepts, highlighted in green, that need to be known and understood. Although there are no comparative questions for the unit, reference is made to comparative features in the UK political system, to facilitate the synoptic understanding required at A2. While making no claim to cover every possible aspect of the four specification areas in detail, the content guidance aims to provide concise but thorough coverage of the core topics. This material is best used as the basis for further in-depth study and your own independent research to find additional examples and evidence from other sources and from contemporary developments in the ever-changing politics of the USA.

The electoral process and direct democracy

The US electoral process operates in the context of the following constitutional provisions:

- a federal structure, with different layers of government
- a separation of powers, with different branches of government
- fixed terms of office for all elected positions

These can only be changed by constitutional amendment. This system results in 'permanent' campaigns and a sense of 'democratic overload', with more than 100,000 elections taking place annually in over 80,000 units of government, for a wide range of posts from the president to the local dog-catcher.

In the USA, candidates for office are not chosen by the parties, but by voters in primaries and caucuses. This is the nomination process, which takes place every 4 years for the presidential election and every 2 years for the mid-term congressional elections.

What is a caucus?

Caucuses are a series of state-based meetings of party activists who come together to indicate their preferences for the candidates. They are found in less densely populated states, such as Nevada. The caucus in Iowa is the first and is traditionally regarded as the most important, because of the momentum it gives to the winning candidate, as was the case, for example, with Barack Obama in 2008.

Before the 1960s, most states held caucuses, but now only a minority do. Caucus voters are likely to be more extreme activists (to the left in the Democratic Party and to the right in the Republican Party), operating in the 'smoke-filled room' style of

> **Knowledge check 1**
>
> How does the constitutional federal structure and separation of powers affect the US electoral process?

> **momentum** Nicknamed the 'big mo', momentum refers to surges in support after wins in the invisible primary, early primaries and caucuses. It can lead to advantages over rivals, such as more media attention, name and face recognition, donors, voters 'jumping on the bandwagon' and often front-runner status. Candidates who fail to achieve or sustain momentum may drop out early.

machine politics. Caucuses, therefore, are less democratic than primaries. Caucus results are not representative of the opinions of the wider party or electorate, and turnout tends to be very low. Until 1968, it was possible to win the nomination, as Democratic contender Hubert Humphrey did, by winning the support of caucus delegates and ignoring the primaries. This changed after the McGovern–Fraser reforms in the Democratic Party, which expanded participation in the nomination process.

What is a primary?

Primaries are intra-party state elections to select the party's nominee for the presidential election, and are now held in the majority of states. Rules for their use are decided by the states themselves and also by the Democratic and Republican parties within those states. Like caucuses, primaries do not actually elect the candidate, but select delegates to attend the national nominating convention, where they will cast their votes for the winning candidate. The winner of the popular vote in the state primary receives delegates by a winner-takes-all process or by some form of proportional representation, depending on state and party rules. The larger states have more delegates and are therefore important to win.

It is important to note the following points related to the use of state primaries:

- **Open and closed primaries.** In an open primary, any voter can vote in either party's primary (but not in both), while in a closed primary only registered party voters may participate.
- **The invisible primary.** This is the period after candidates declare their intention to run and before the first actual primary, when candidates try to achieve advantages over their rivals such as greater name and face recognition, funding and momentum.
- **Front-loading.** This is the term used when states bring forward their primaries in an attempt to achieve more influence over the outcome.
- **The New Hampshire primary.** New Hampshire is famous as the first state to hold its primary and for the momentum this can give to candidates despite its small and unrepresentative character. Until Bill Clinton in 1992, every president had won this primary, but since then it has not been a reliable predictor of the winner. George W. Bush did not win it in 2000, and Obama lost to Hillary Clinton in 2008.
- **Super Tuesday.** The southern states realised that their overall voice would be more significant if they could create a front-runner candidate by holding their primaries on the same day. In 2008, on 'Super-duper Tuesday', 16 primary states voted on the same day with this aim.

What is the case *for* the use of primaries?

- Primaries provide more democratic choice for voters, ending 'smoke-filled room' politics and control by party bosses who are not representative of the wider party.
- They show who can win and where. Primaries produce candidates with national appeal who can win in different regions of the country. For example, Clinton in 1992 was a southern Democrat who showed he had appeal in the northern liberal states, while John Kerry in 2004 and Obama in 2008 were northern liberals who showed that they could win in the conservative south.

Knowledge check 2

Which kinds of state hold caucuses, who votes in them and with what results?

Knowledge check 3

What is the significance of the invisible primary?

Examiner tip

The reasons for the use of state primaries and caucuses, their characteristics and their outcomes are different, so always use examples of the results of primaries and caucuses to provide evidence of differences.

- Primaries weed out weaker candidates with little chance of winning the presidential election: such candidates fail to gain or sustain momentum as the primary campaigns progress.
- The long and gruelling nature of the primaries tests the stamina and character of the candidates and therefore their suitability for the presidency.

What is the case *against* the use of primaries?

- They go on for too long. The invisible primary effectively creates a situation of permanent campaigning, which causes many voters to lose interest.
- The constant media focus tends to trivialise the process, emphasising 'beauty contest' image rather than 'policy' substance.
- The huge cost of campaigning means that candidates spend an excessive amount of time fund-raising. Candidates who lack funds or face a well-financed rival may have to drop out, regardless of their qualities as potential presidents.
- Candidates can become exhausted by relentless travelling and campaigning under a 24/7 media spotlight, particularly when they already hold demanding political office.
- Primaries can give momentum to **'outsider' candidates** with little experience of governing and no substantial preparation for the presidency. (This does not necessarily mean, of course, that such a candidate will not make a good president.)
- Primaries reduce the party's role in selecting its presidential nominee, as candidates create personal campaign organisations, raise finance and run on their personality and views, with little peer review from party insiders.
- Primaries are divisive contests, as candidates from the same party attack and try to discredit each other, making it difficult to reunite the party to fight the real contest in November. This happened in 1992 to the Republican Party and George Bush lost the subsequent election.
- Because of low turnout, primaries can lead to unrepresentative results.
- To win primaries, Republican candidates must move to the right to appeal to their base of core voters, whereas Democratic candidates must move to the left. They then have to pull the campaign back into the middle ground to fight the real election, thus potentially alienating voters.

How important are the national nominating conventions?

The national nominating conventions are slick media spectacles run by the parties' national committees, and they conclude the nomination process. They have become less important in recent years, as the primaries now decide the nominee — at the convention, committed state delegates vote for the candidate who won their state primary (or caucus). As a result, the main role of the national nominating convention is now to 'crown' the candidate rather than to choose the candidate, as it did in the past.

Although the conventions have lost their formal function to decide the parties' presidential nominees, they retain several important informal functions:

Knowledge check 4

Why have primaries been described as 'political Darwinism?'

Examiner tip

There is no agreement on whether the use of primaries or caucuses is the best process to select the presidential candidates. Understand the debate over both the democratic advantages and the disadvantages of these selection methods.

outsider candidates

This term refers to a candidate's lack of experience of Washington DC politics. Many outsider candidates are state governors who 'run against Washington politics' such as Jimmy Carter, Ronald Reagan and George W. Bush. Insiders like George Bush stress Washington experience of how the system works. Outsider candidates like Bill Clinton may choose a Washington insider to balance the ticket, such as Senator Al Gore.

Knowledge check 5

Why do 'political wounds' have to be healed at the conventions?

Knowledge check 6

Explain the role of the super-delegates in the Democratic Party.

Examiner tip

See the importance of the conventions in ending the nomination process in the states and launching the national campaign, and be able to distinguish between their formal and informal functions.

balanced ticket
Presidential nominees wish to select a vice-president with different characteristics from their own to maximise their vote by appealing to different types of voter. The ticket can be balanced ideologically, geographically, ethnically or by factors such as gender, age, religion or experience. Each choice will show different factors at work.

Knowledge check 7

Give examples of the 'specialist advisers' who run presidential campaigns.

- The convention ratifies the party's official nominee, and after the acceptance speech the party has the opportunity to unite around the chosen candidate and heal political wounds from the campaign — as happened in 2008 but not in 1992.
- The convention is the only time the party meets nationally, bringing together delegates from 50 state parties and the party's super-delegates — the party officials and elected representatives who are not pledged or bound by primary or caucus votes. After the convention, the party effectively reverts to 50 state parties.
- The party platform, its official set of policy positions, is adopted at the national nominating convention, in a way similar (but not identical) to the adoption of a party manifesto in the UK. These platform policies will already have been put forward in the winning candidate's primary campaign, so in effect the convention is now endorsing them rather than determining them.
- The presidential candidate hopes to achieve a 'bounce' in the polls after the convention as a result of extensive media coverage and a national platform.
- Historically, the vice-presidential nominee was chosen at the convention, but now the choice of running mate is announced before it. The office of vice-president is seen as relatively insignificant, but the choice of nominee is important for providing a **balanced ticket** — the vice-presidential nominee will have characteristics not possessed by the presidential candidate, which it is hoped will widen their appeal to voters. Obama's selection of Biden in 2008 balanced his race, age and lack of Washington experience, and was aimed at attracting the white, male, blue-collar vote. McCain's controversial choice of Governor Palin gave gender and age balance as well as pleasing the party's social conservative base.

The choice of the 'veep' is regarded by some as a rather haphazard event, given that the person chosen will be, as is often said, only 'a heartbeat away from the presidency'.

What are the key features of the presidential campaign?

Once the balloons come down on delegates at the end of the nominating convention, the candidate and party gear up for the national campaign, starting officially on Labor Day, the first Monday in September.

In the presidential campaign, the candidate must try to influence more than 200 million voters, in 50 states of variable electoral importance. They will target their campaign strategy, aided by armies of specialist advisers whose job is to help them win the biggest prize, control of the executive branch of government. To do this they must:

- 'energise the base': enthuse their core, aligned voters to turn out to vote
- win over the independent voters whose votes are not yet decided — a difficult balancing act
- create momentum for the campaign by raising funds and creating an electoral bandwagon

In their campaign strategy, they must take into account the following factors:

- The huge size of the USA and the diversity of the voters.

- The need to win Electoral College votes by focusing on key 'swing states' such as Ohio, Florida and Pennsylvania, ruthlessly targeting them with campaign funds and political advertising. Candidates will tend to ignore states they know they can win and those they are bound to lose.
- The need to target 'swing voters' in key states, such as the elderly in Florida or industrial workers in Ohio, with specific messages. At the same time they must target the women's vote, the youth vote, the Hispanic vote and other groups, which can cause problems in terms of what to say, where and to whom in order to win votes (or not lose them).
- Candidates can no longer rely on large numbers of aligned voters always turning out to vote for their party.
- The 'incumbency effect'. An incumbent president can have an advantage through being perceived as looking more 'presidential' than the challenger. This did not, however, help incumbents Jimmy Carter in 1980 and George H. W. Bush in 1992, when other factors were important in explaining their defeat. (This effect is more significant in congressional elections, where incumbent senators and representatives can gain significant electoral advantage by, for example, claiming credit for securing federal funding for local 'pork-barrel' projects.)

Candidates make appeals to voters on the basis of:

- the party identification of the voters: the candidate's Democratic or Republican label is the voting cue for aligned voters
- their personal characteristics, such as likeability or trustworthiness, and their experience: voters often vote for the candidate rather than for the party, and it was said that George W. Bush's defeat of John Kerry in 2004 was partly due to voters thinking he was more of a 'regular guy'
- the policy positions that they take on important salient political issues, especially on the economy

Finally, candidates attempt to connect with voters and persuade them through:

- old-style whistle-stop campaigns, visiting key states and making speeches
- the great debates on television
- focus groups
- political advertising through the mass media and modern technology such as the internet

In order to win the presidency, candidates must use the above to build broad coalitions of voters, who will vote through the medium of the Electoral College, within the fixed terms laid down by the constitution.

How important are the media in election campaigns?

The mass media are now the main channel of political communication enabling candidates to connect to voters. The first election in which television was a major factor was in 1960, when John Kennedy's television image was seen as the key factor in his success over the less media-friendly Richard Nixon.

swing states Also called 'battleground states', these are states that can be won or lost by either candidate, unlike red (Democrat) or blue (Republican) 'safe states'. There are around ten swing states where small movements of votes could turn a state from blue to red or vice versa, effectively deciding the result. Candidates focus their campaigns in these states with constant advertising and frequent visits.

Examiner tip
Make sure you can identify and explain the key strategies that drive US election campaigns and what is needed to win.

The media have four main influences on campaigns:

- The media personalise campaigns, tending to focus on image and appearance rather than policy positions, on style rather than substance. It is said that Abraham Lincoln's appearance would make him unelectable in modern politics. It is also argued that media focus changes the types of candidate coming forward, as well as their style of campaigning. Candidates are marketed on the basis of their looks, personalities and personal views, with little focus on the party in whose name they stand.

- Elections are now held under 24/7 media coverage. Campaigns are run by experienced media advisers and pollsters who use focus groups and 'voter meters' to test voter reaction to candidates and what they are saying. Candidates will often shift their views in response to professional consultations with key groups in the electorate.

- There is increasing emphasis on photo-opportunities on prime-time television, often engineered to get coverage in the free media, such as news channels like Fox, CNN and MSBNC, rather than relying on the paid media of television advertising. Candidates compete to coin the best soundbites to capture the attention of the electorate, such as Obama's 'Yes we can.' Everything is planned to come across well on television, which helps candidates who are good media performers, such as Ronald Reagan, but can damage those who aren't, such as Gore in 2000 and McCain in 2008.

- Cable networks are used to send highly targeted messages in order to influence groups of voters. For example, the Christian Broadcasting Network can influence religious voters on issues such as abortion or gay marriage, while the conservative 'shock jock' radio channels can influence voters on the right.

The influence of television advertising on the campaign

- Buying television advertising time is very expensive, and this is the main reason why candidates need to raise huge amounts of campaign finance.
- What is seen or heard in the media rarely persuades voters to switch their vote, but it reinforces views the voter already has. Advertising is therefore used to 'energise the base' rather than to attempt to convert votes.
- There is increasing use of **negative campaigning**, especially 'attack ads' — advertisements attacking opponents rather than putting forward positive messages. Although it is widely criticised, the reason why negative campaigning is used is that it works and is hard to counteract. It often involves painting opponents as extremist or unpatriotic. A notable example was the damaging Swift Boat Veterans for Truth advert used against Kerry in 2004, questioning his patriotism and bravery in the Vietnam War. There was, however, less evidence of successful negative advertising in 2008, despite attempts to portray Obama as 'un-American', probably because of the important issues dominating the campaign. Negative advertising may be linked to the increasingly partisan nature of the American media.

How important are the 'great debates'?

The term used for the face-to-face broadcast encounters between the two rival candidates is a misnomer since they are arguably neither great nor debates. The first was in 1960, between John F. Kennedy, who was deemed to have won by the television

Knowledge check 8

Explain what is meant by the term 'personalised campaigns'.

Knowledge check 9

Explain the difference between the 'paid media' and the 'free media'.

negative campaigning
This is where a campaign's strategists attack and discredit their opponent's character and policies rather than positively campaigning on the candidate's own merits and policies. It is debatable whether it helps mobilise partisan core voters, alienates independent voters or both. Most campaigns 'go negative' when losing support or when there are few policy issues dividing the candidates.

viewers, and Richard Nixon, who was deemed to have won by the radio listeners, which suggests that in the end image can trump what is actually said.

The debates are now hugely stage-managed and the candidates try to score points against each other. There is evidence that voters watching the 'debates' respond to style rather than substance, as they did in 1960, judging which candidate has the most presidential appearance. A good performance, however, can create a bounce in the polls, while a mistake can damage a candidate's image and momentum, and bring them down in the polls. The debates are more likely to reinforce than to change the views of voters.

Campaign finance

It is said in the USA that 'money doesn't talk, it shouts', and that 'America has the best democracy money can buy', such is the crucial role of money in the electoral process. A vital factor in a candidate's success in the primaries is whether he or she can amass a huge campaign war chest. This gives them a major advantage over less well-financed candidates, but also works to deter challengers who cannot raise the finance to make or sustain a bid for the presidency.

Why is money so important in US campaigns?

Finance is important in electoral campaigns for a number of reasons, including:

- the high cost of television advertising to reach voters
- the size of the country and consequently the high costs of travel and accommodation in 50 states
- the diversity of voters to whom the candidates have to appeal with highly targeted messages
- the need to hire specialist staff to run a modern campaign, including the use of new technology
- the permanent nature of campaigning, with the build-up for the next election starting the day after the last one ends

Where do candidates get their campaign finance from?

Candidates' finance comes primarily from:

- their own pockets — so it helps to be a multi-millionaire
- political action committees (PACs)
- national and congressional party committees
- 527 groups and Super PACs raising money to spend on issue advocacy on behalf of candidates
- fund-raising through the internet and social media, generating large numbers of small donations, as practised with great success by the Obama campaign in 2008

The Federal Election Campaign Act

The context for the contemporary debate on the role of finance in electoral success dates from reforms in the 1970s, when the Watergate scandal revealed financial corruption in donations to candidates. There was a view that elections were for sale to the highest bidder, and that in financial terms the candidates did not have a level playing field.

Knowledge check 10

Why are candidates now likely to reject federal funding for their campaigns?

The Federal Election Campaign Act (FECA) of 1971 and later amendments introduced federal funding for presidential (but not congressional) elections, with matching funds provided for candidates in the primaries who could raise lots of small contributions in at least 20 states, helping serious but outsider candidates such as Jimmy Carter in 1976 and Bill Clinton in 1992 to gain funds.

Federal funding is offered to each presidential candidate. If a candidate accepts federal funds, as John McCain did in 2008, they must agree to spending limits on their campaign. Alternatively, if they want to raise unlimited amounts of money to spend on their campaign, they can choose to reject federal funding, as Barack Obama did in 2008.

As a result of FECA, all contributions to candidates must be disclosed and supervised by the Federal Election Commission (FEC), making the process open and transparent. Also, limits are placed on all direct contributions to candidates, the so-called **hard money** of US politics.

hard money Regulated money, contributed directly to a candidate, subject to limits, monitored by the Federal Election Commission and intended to prevent the 'buying' of elections.

What was the impact of the FECA reforms on election campaigns?

Federal funding went to candidates not parties, weakening the latter's role in campaigning and strengthening the personalised nature of the campaign. The reforms also reinforced the two-party system, as minor parties usually fail to achieve the 5% share of the vote at the previous election necessary to receive federal funding.

Advantages remain for rich candidates who can spend as much of their own money as they wish on their campaign. The 1976 Supreme Court judgment *Buckley* v *Valeo* ruled parts of FECA unconstitutional, as freedom to spend money expressing political opinions could not be denied under the 1st Amendment.

The Bipartisan Campaign Reform Act 2002 (McCain–Feingold)

Money in politics is like water on an old roof: it will always find a way through. The rising cost of US campaigns was widely criticised as multi-million-dollar campaigns increased, making politics look like the preserve of the rich and special interests, who were accused of 'buying' elections. The main loophole in the control of campaign finance was through **soft money** — unregulated money that found its way into the campaign, including 'independent expenditures' where individuals or organisations could spend 'on behalf of' candidates through 'issue advocacy': for example, funding a pro-gun advert that would indirectly benefit one candidate but without directly donating to the campaign or directly promoting a candidate. Another soft money loophole was that large donations could be given to the parties for 'general political activities', such as 'get out the vote' efforts, but was often used for supporting party electoral candidates, especially in tight races.

soft money Unregulated money, usually given to parties for 'general political activities', but banned in 2002. It now refers to money not subject to FECA restrictions or limits, usually given to groups for 'issue advocacy'.

In 2002, however, the McCain–Feingold Bipartisan Campaign Reform Act (BCRA) was passed, which banned all soft money contributions to candidates or parties and increased the upper limit for hard money donations from individuals to $2,000 (now $2,500).

One result of this Act was to change campaign finance strategy, and candidates now make internet appeals to large numbers of small donors, making greater use of grass-roots fund-raising activities.

BCRA led indirectly to the growth of '527 groups', named after a section of the US tax code which allows organisations to raise and spend unlimited amounts of money for 'general political activities', although they are not allowed to coordinate their activities (usually television advertising) with the candidate or party they are supporting. A famous example of the 527s was the Swift Boat Veterans for Truth group, which funded an advert attacking Kerry's war record of bravery in order to neutralise his advantage over Bush (an alleged draft dodger). The ad was aired almost constantly and effectively in key states before the 2004 election.

FEC v Citizens United and the new 'Super PACs'

This controversial 5/4 decision by the Supreme Court in January 2010, based on the free speech provisions of the 1st Amendment, blew a huge hole in attempts to regulate campaign spending by law.

The decision allows corporations, unions and individuals to make unlimited donations to partisan groups, now known as Super PACs, which then campaign for or against electoral candidates. (Unlike traditional PACs, they cannot directly donate any hard money to candidates.) The decision has led to an even greater influx of special interest money in campaigns, such as the spending of $75 million in 2010 by the US Chamber of Commerce to target for defeat lawmakers who had voted for healthcare reform. Much of this money is spent on financing 'attack advertising' on TV (although candidates now have personally to endorse TV ads made to support them). For example, the new Super PAC American Crossroads, associated with Karl Rove, spent $70 million supporting Republican candidates and opposing Democrats in the 2010 mid-term elections.

Although the new Super PACs can receive and spend unlimited amounts of money, they cannot coordinate their spending with either parties or candidates, but can spend 'on behalf of' them using 'independent expenditures' for 'issue advocacy'. Obama has described them as a 'threat to democracy' because of the increasing amount of money spent by them in campaigns and their likely influence over campaign outcomes. Another criticism is that, although Super PACs must disclose their donors to the FEC, there is a loophole which allows the groups to link with advocacy groups such as the new '501(c) 4' groups (also named after a section of the tax code) which can raise unlimited amounts of money to spend supporting or opposing candidates, but which do not have to disclose their donors.

A key question in US politics is whether candidates, or special interests who spend on their behalf, can 'buy' electoral success and also whether well-funded candidates have an unfair advantage over poorer rivals: there are arguments on both sides of the debate. It is possible to find very rich candidates who have lost, and the best-financed candidate does not always win, especially in congressional contests. There are several other factors that are important in a candidate's electoral success, such as their policies, record and image, and the circumstances of the time. Another question is whether, in a country with rights guaranteed by the constitution's 1st Amendment, it could ever be possible to limit campaign spending effectively by law.

Examiner tip

Make sure you are up to date with all recent changes to campaign finance laws and Supreme Court decisions in this area.

Examiner tip

The Centre for Responsive Politics website www.opensecrets.org and www.fec.gov provide excellent, up-to-date campaign finance statistics to use as evidence of campaign spending and its effects.

Knowledge check 11

Why does the 1st Amendment limit any attempt to control spiralling campaign finance?

What is the Electoral College and how does it work?

- The Electoral College is a constitutional mechanism designed to 'filter the people's will' and to elect the president indirectly. It was the result of a compromise reached in 1787, when large and small states disagreed over how the president should be elected.
- Candidates need to win the Electoral College vote, not necessarily the popular vote, to become president.
- Electoral College votes are allocated to states according to their congressional representation: the two senators from each state plus the number of congressional districts within the state, which reflects the size of the state's population. This means the states with smaller populations have few Electoral College votes (seven states have only 3 votes) and the larger states have more. Florida in 2012 will have 29 (+2) and New York 29 (–2), while California still has 55 Electoral College votes.
- Demographic change means states can lose Electoral College votes through declining population, and re-districting can reduce the number of districts in the state, as in New York. They can also, of course, gain Electoral College votes if the opposite happens, as in Florida. States therefore become more or less important because of this.
- The total number of Electoral College votes is fixed at 538, made up of 100 votes from Senate representation, 435 from House representation and 3 from Washington DC.
- Candidates need 270 Electoral College votes to win, and these can be gained in many different ways.
- The last deadlocked vote in the Electoral College was in 1824, but the potential for a 269–269 vote is always there.
- The Electoral College follows a winner-takes-all system. In the majority of states the winner of the popular vote takes all that state's Electoral College votes regardless of the margin of the vote. Thus if a candidate wins the popular vote in Ohio with a vote of 51% they get all of Ohio's 18 Electoral College votes. Only Maine and Nebraska allocate their Electoral College votes proportionally. Voters actually vote for a slate of electors who will deliver their votes in the state capital the following month.
- The device of the Electoral College is linked to federalism, as a presidential election is actually 50 separate contests in the 50 states (plus Washington DC) on the same day.

What are the effects of the Electoral College on the campaign?

The main effect of the Electoral College system is on the campaign strategies of candidates: they will usually concentrate on the 'swing' battleground states, especially those with large Electoral College votes, rather than the ones they either can't win or can't lose. Candidates rarely campaign in every state (as Nixon did in 1960, losing to Kennedy, who won seven of the eight largest Electoral College vote states by a hair's breadth) and they often ignore large parts of the country and large numbers of voters when campaigning. This can lead to differences in turnout, as voters in some states

Knowledge check 12

How can a presidential candidate lose the popular vote yet win the presidential election, as happened in 2000?

Examiner tip

You must be clear and precise when explaining how and why the Electoral College works the way it does, always using accurate figures as evidence.

lack an incentive to vote. Candidates focus on key swing voters in swing states, such as the elderly in Florida or blue-collar voters in Pennsylvania, in order to win.

What criticisms are made of the Electoral College and its outcomes?

- A candidate losing the national popular vote may win the Electoral College vote, as Bush did in 2000. This puts the president's mandate and legitimacy in question, as it can be seen as denying the people's will.
- The winner-takes-all system means that all Electoral College votes go to the winner in a state (with the exception of Maine and Nebraska) regardless of the narrowness of the victory.
- Campaign promises tend to be targeted on swing voters in swing states to the exclusion of other 'less important' voters in safe states.
- Both the small and the large states are over-represented in the final vote.
- Third-party candidates can only win Electoral College votes with a concentrated vote in a state or states, as George Wallace did in 1968 when he won five southern states. Ross Perot's 19% national share of the vote in 1992 brought him nothing, as his vote was too dispersed to win states.
- There is a possibility of 'faithless' or 'rogue' electors. State electors are pledged but not constitutionally bound to vote for the winner of the popular vote. There are occasions when individual electors do not do this, usually because they wish to make some political point. This is also seen as a denial of the people's will. Normally such behaviour would not make a difference to the outcome, but in a deadlocked Electoral College of 269–269 it could do so.

Why has the Electoral College not been changed?

- The Electoral College system has provided political stability by electing a president with a clear majority and mandate in all but three presidential elections since the eighteenth century. The result in 2000 was an aberration.
- Demands for reform run up against the strength of the Electoral College's constitutional status and tradition. Any change is subject to a constitutional amendment, which would require super-majorities for success. In the event of a deadlocked Electoral College, there is already a contingency plan whereby the decision on who will be president is given to the House of Representatives (with the Senate deciding the vice-president).
- There is strong self-interest on the part of states which benefit from the workings of the Electoral College. Smaller states are over-represented in terms of their population, and larger states have their needs addressed because of their voting power, so there is no incentive for either to seek change.
- There is little public pressure for reform, and no consensus on an acceptable alternative for electing the president. A direct popular vote conflicts with the federal nature of the USA and the jealously guarded rights of the individual states.
- The working of the Electoral College is one reason for the USA's two-party duopoly, with all presidents being Democrat or Republican. The USA has a single-person executive, so there are no demands for proportional representation, unlike the UK, where the electoral system elects a government. It would require exceptional circumstances for a third party to have a significant effect on the outcome.

Knowledge check 13
How significant are 'faithless' or 'rogue' electors?

Examiner tip
Know about the Electoral College results for at least two presidential elections and be able to use the Electoral College vote, the popular vote and any 'rogue electors' as evidence.

Examiner tip
The Electoral College can be both criticised and defended. There is no agreement on whether it should be retained, reformed or replaced. You should know the key debates over the advantages and disadvantages of these options.

Knowledge check 14
Explain the link between federalism and the retention of the Electoral College.

As a result, despite several valid criticisms, it is unlikely that the Electoral College will be reformed or abolished. To paraphrase Churchill on democracy, it could be said that 'The Electoral College is the worst way of electing the president, except for all the rest.'

The use of direct democracy in the USA

Although the USA has never held a national referendum, there are provisions for direct democracy mechanisms in some states, dating from the early-twentieth-century progressive era. These mechanisms were seen as a way of extending democracy, putting trust in people to make decisions affecting their lives. They supplement representative democracy, but do not replace it.

What is the difference between referendums and initiatives?

Referendums

Referendums are devices used to refer a specific question directly to voters. In some states, a measure passed in the state legislature does not come into effect unless it is given approval in a referendum by voters. They are therefore a top-down device which allows a decision to receive demonstrable popular approval and greater legitimacy. All states (except Delaware) have a requirement that amendments to the state constitution be approved by referendum. They are also frequently used for bond issues as a way of raising money for state finances.

Initiatives

In some states, the device of initiatives allows citizens to initiate a proposed state law or change in the law, provided the required number of voter signatures is collected to support it through petitions (usually between 5% and 15% of the voters in a state). If this is achieved, the question (proposition) will be placed on the ballot at an election for registered voters to support or reject. Initiatives are bottom-up devices initiated by citizens, not legislators. If supported by a majority vote, the result is usually binding on the state legislature, but many successful initiatives are struck down in the courts after legal challenges. Many think it ironic that voters elect representatives to make decisions on their behalf in the classic Burkeian sense, but then bypass those elected representatives through the initiative process. There are hundreds of examples of initiative questions: they are often on moral issues such as gay marriage or abortion, but also apply to many other political issues, such as property taxes, gun control or affirmative action. There were 103 ballot initiatives in 2008.

The use of initiatives has been increasing as controversial and divisive issues have grown and voters lack confidence in their state legislators to take decisions on them. It is also now easier to consult the people, thanks to technological advances. Pressure groups see initiatives as a good way of getting their views across to voters, allowing them to take action on these single issues that goes beyond the 'blanket vote' they have at elections.

Arguments *for* the use of direct democracy

- Referendums and initiatives are said to express the will of the people and are the purest form of democracy.

Examiner tip
Note that questions on direct democracy may relate to referendums and/or initiatives and/or recall elections, and the three should be clearly distinguished.

Knowledge check 15
What is meant by saying that direct democracy 'supplements but does not replace' representative democracy?

Knowledge check 16
What is meant by the descriptions 'bottom up' and 'top down' in the context of the use of direct democracy?

Examiner tip
Have at least three well-researched examples of successful initiatives being passed in the USA to use as evidence in your answers.

- Voters vote to get what they want, not what their representatives think they should get.
- Referendums and initiatives encourage wider political participation and engagement with issues.
- Voters are educated on issues as views for and against are debated in campaigns through the media.

Arguments *against* the use of direct democracy

- Elected representatives make decisions after informed debates in legislatures, using their judgement as to what is best for all the people in the long term. If you don't like their decisions you can vote to remove them at the next election.
- Voters tend to vote for their own short-term interests, as in the vote to reduce property taxes in Proposition 13 in California in 1978.
- Initiatives can threaten minority rights, such as the abolition of gay marriage rights in Proposition 8 in California in 2008.
- Initiatives can be passed on the basis of small, unrepresentative turnouts of fickle voters influenced by emotive and well-financed media and pressure group campaigns.
- Campaigns lead to oversimplified arguments on highly complex issues to which only a yes/no answer can be given.
- The initiative process can be manipulated by wealthy pressure groups, employing consultants to initiate the proposition and raise the signatures to put it on the ballot. Most initiatives are not initiated by ordinary citizens, but by special interest groups wanting to influence decisions in their favour.
- The opposing sides may have unequal resources and media time, which can prevent fair representation of competing opinions. Studies show the highest-spending side usually wins, while the result may only benefit special interest groups rather than the wider community.

Some political scientists argue strongly in favour of the use of initiatives, whereas others are equally strongly against. It depends who is thought most likely to make the best decisions on public policies: the people themselves or their elected and accountable representatives.

What are recall elections?

The recall election appears to be a highly democratic device, allowing registered voters to recall an elected state or local official from office once a signature petition and evidence of corrupt or incompetent behaviour have been presented. In 2003 Gray Davis, the Democratic Governor of California, was recalled by 55% of the electorate and replaced by Arnold Schwarzenegger, who defeated 130 other candidates to win the recall election. There are no federal recall elections, and they are rare in the states.

The key argument in favour of recall elections is that they make elected officials more accountable to citizens between elections and more responsive to the public's wishes. The key argument against is that the recall may be politically motivated, aimed at removing a serving politician who was not defeated in a democratic contest at the previous election.

Examiner tip

There is no agreement on the benefits of using direct democracy devices as supplements to representative democracy in some US states. Be prepared both to defend and to attack both direct and representative democracy as ways of making public policy decisions.

Examiner tip

Study the recall of Governor Gray Davis in California in 2003 in order to understand the arguments both in favour of and against the recall process.

Knowledge check 17

How are direct democracy mechanisms triggered in the states that use them?

Some comparative features of UK electoral processes

- The 1911 Parliament Act set a maximum 5-year term for Parliament, but within that limit the prime minister has chosen when to go to the country. However, as a result of new legislation the UK will have fixed-term parliaments, avoiding the governing party having an advantage through control of the election date.
- The general election is for the election of MPs only; there is no separate election of the prime minister, and the government is drawn from the majority party in a parliamentary system.
- Constituency parties choose candidates and can also deselect them.
- The party leader is elected by the parliamentary party and the mass membership (and trade unions in the Labour Party).
- There is no equivalent to the national nominating conventions, although parties hold annual conferences.
- The campaign is a national one, fought by parties with manifestos in an official 3-week campaign.
- Campaign finance is legally limited and parties cannot buy political advertising on television. Time is allocated free of charge for party election broadcasts.
- All referendums on constitutional issues have been initiated by government. There is no provision for initiatives or recall elections in the UK.

Examiner tip

Do not introduce long, artificial and especially irrelevant UK references into your answers, although they may be used in passing to show you understand differences between elections and direct democracy in both countries.

Summary

After studying this topic you should be able to:

- Put the US electoral process and direct democracy into the constitutional context of federalism, fixed terms, separation of powers and the Electoral College, which explains, in many ways, why it works the way it does.
- Understand the US electoral process as a continuous process from the invisible primary through to the results of the Electoral College vote.
- Explain the main features of the nomination process, including the invisible primary, the primary and caucus systems and their outcomes, as well as the role and importance of the national nominating conventions.
- Understand the main features of the election campaigns of the candidates, and the main factors influencing the outcome of the campaign and the success of the candidates.
- Recognise the crucial importance of campaign finance in US elections, including how candidates raise their money, what they spend it on, the changes made to it and whether it is always a significant factor in explaining a candidate's success.
- Identify and explain the workings of the Electoral College system to elect the president and why it

has been retained despite several criticisms, and not abolished and replaced or fundamentally reformed.

- Explain the workings of different kinds of direct democracy found in some US states and the arguments both for and against their use.
- Make references to the UK electoral process and direct democracy where relevant.
- Recognise the key debates and competing arguments in all these areas, including:
  - whether primaries and caucuses and nominating conventions are the best way of selecting the presidential candidates for the parties
  - whether money actually is the most important factor in a candidate's electoral success and whether the focus on fund-raising and huge financial war chests distorts the democratic process and allows the 'buying' of elections
  - whether the Electoral College remains the best way of electing the president of the United States
  - whether direct democracy is a better way of making political decisions than representative democracy

Political parties

Political parties are organisations of like-minded people who come together in order to win political power, so that they can put their ideologies into effect and achieve their collective policy goals. In America, the Founding Fathers were suspicious of parties, but factions coalesced into the Federalists and Anti-Federalists and a two-party system was born. These factions later developed into the Democratic and Republican parties, demonstrating an ability to reinvent themselves in response to changing circumstances which continues to this day.

The two US parties have often been described as similar, not least because of their broad political consensus on:

- the constitution and the political system it created
- a capitalist economic system, with (greater or lesser) commitment to private enterprise and free markets
- the 'dominant ideology' in the USA, with (greater or lesser) commitment to individualism, liberty, equality and the American Dream

The two parties are also described as pragmatic, 'big tent', catch-all internal coalitions, whose aim at elections is to maximise their vote in order to gain office rather than to put into practice an ideological blueprint or 'ism'. It is alleged that they usually operate in the middle ground of politics, rarely straying out of this comfort zone. When they do move outside the mainstream they are heavily defeated, as was the case with the very conservative Republican Barry Goldwater in 1964 and the very liberal Democrat George McGovern in 1972. The lesson learnt from these defeats was that parties must build broad coalitions of voting support to achieve electoral success.

This leads to criticisms, particularly in the past, that US parties offer 'fudged' positions without giving a clear choice to voters, creating the impression that they simply want to get into government rather than offering a coherent policy programme.

The old view that the two main US parties are almost indistinguishable, however, is now very oversimplified. There are many differences between them in terms of:

- their ideologies, values and policies (what they believe in and do)
- their voting support (who supports them and why)

The parties do offer some choice to voters: this is greater or lesser at different elections, depending on who the candidates are and which issues are dominant.

How do the parties differ?

The Democratic Party

Historically the party of the South and the pro-slavery, anti-Union party, it became the majority party from the 1930s when Roosevelt's New Deal programme led to *realignment* in US politics. The party won support from a new coalition of votes, the New Deal Coalition, which involved two contradictory kinds of voter. It gained support from a 'northern wing' of minorities, urban blue-collar workers, trade unionists and liberal intellectuals. At the same time it retained support from its 'southern wing' of white segregationist,

> **Examiner tip**
> Be aware that although the parties have at times appeared similar, operating in the middle ground of politics, this view of US parties has had some important readjustments, particularly since the 1980s.

> **Knowledge check 18**
> What is meant in politics by the term 'realignment'?

conservative voters who strongly identified with the party that had supported slavery and the Confederacy. The strength of this voting support made the party the 'natural party of government' from the 1930s to the 1960s, when the New Deal Coalition finally broke down under the strain of holding such contradictory voting blocs together. The breaking point came after the 1964 Civil Rights and 1965 Voting Rights legislation when, as Lyndon Johnson stated at the time, the party 'signed away the South'.

Since the 1960s, the Democratic Party has only managed to win the presidency with southern candidates — Carter in 1976 and Clinton in 1992 and 1996 — but this changed with Obama's win in 2008.

What does the Democratic Party believe in?

liberalism An ideological leaning on the centre left of the political spectrum in the USA (but not left wing as in socialism). The term was first used in the 1930s to describe support for the New Deal and voters and politicians who are more politically progressive, supporting change and intervention in the political and economic system to improve citizens' lives, and creating greater equality and social justice.

The Democratic Party is the more liberal party, associated with:

- a more activist, interventionist government role in regulating and managing the economy in the interests of all the people
- the introduction and development of social welfare programmes such as Medicare/ Medicaid in healthcare to promote greater equality
- equal rights programmes such as civil rights, women's rights and gay rights
- commitment to federal rather than state government action
- a more 'dovish' foreign policy, internationalist in seeking diplomatic solutions to problems
- a more 'pro-choice' stance on abortion and more in favour of gun control, immigration, environmental protection and ending the death penalty

It is because of these ideological views, values and associated policy positions that the Democratic Party attracts voting support from:

- blue-collar workers, trade unionists and less affluent public sector workers attracted by its economic views
- minorities attracted by its commitment to equal rights
- city dwellers in the 'blue' states
- intellectuals and radicals attracted to its liberal agenda
- a majority of female voters in recent elections

However, the Democratic Party lost some of its voting support to the Republicans, from:

- southern white voters in the 1960s because of its commitment to civil rights
- some northern blue-collar voters in the 1970s and 1980s alienated by its perceived liberalism

Knowledge check 19

When and why did the New Deal Coalition of votes for the Democratic Party break down?

The loss of this support meant that the party became a more cohesive and coherent ideologically liberal party, particularly with the shedding of the conservative South from its voting coalition. However, the Democratic Party is still internally divided on some ideological and policy positions.

What are the main divisions in the Democratic Party?

As seen with the New Deal Coalition, the Democratic Party has historically been factionalised, with a clear division into two groups:

- **Its southern, conservative wing**: traditionally, Democrats elected from southern states, holding conservative views on all issues, economic, social and foreign, and never reliable Democrat voters in Congress. The modern equivalent of these 'Dixiecrat' southern Democrats are the Blue Dog Democrats. These more fiscally and/or socially conservative Democrats, representing more conservative districts, numbered 47 in the 2009–11 session of Congress and held the balance of power, with the majority of them voting against the public option in Obama's healthcare reforms, which he was forced to abandon. They were labelled DINOs (Democrats in name only) by liberal Democrats. Many were defeated in the 2010 mid-term elections and there are around 23 members now in the Blue Dog caucus.

- **Its northeastern, liberal wing:** Democrats from more liberal northeastern states and the west coast, such as the late Ted Kennedy and ex-speaker Nancy Pelosi. It is this wing of the party that alienated traditional Democrat voters and allowed the Republican Party to paint it as a tax-and-spend party supporting minorities and liberal ('socialist') causes in 2008 and 2010.

A new grouping developed in the 1980s: the 'New Democrats' (neo-liberals), associated with Bill Clinton, Al Gore and the Democratic Leadership Council. They were the 'modernisers' of the Democratic Party, whose aim was to rid the party of the liberal tax-and-spend image that had damaged its presidential hopes. They wanted to win back the more conservative blue-collar and southern voters who had moved to support the Republican Party from the 1960s to the 1980s, and to win back the presidency, which they did in 1992 and 1996 with southerners Clinton and Gore on the ticket.

Like New Labour in the UK, the Democratic Party focused on regaining the centre ground of US politics by developing 'Third Way politics' and 'triangulation' (cherry-picking popular positions from both left and right), exemplified by Clinton's 1996 statement that 'the era of big government is over' and his restrictive welfare reforms.

After the 2008 election, the Democratic Party again became the majority party in Washington as a result of constructing a new Democratic 'Obama coalition' of votes. However, the party lost its majority in the House in the 2010 mid-term elections, largely through a low turnout of its own voters and an energised Republican vote, demonstrating that no real realignment had taken place.

The Republican Party

The Republican Party, or GOP (Grand Old Party), is historically associated with northern, pro-Union, anti-slavery views. It was the majority party until the 1930s, when realignment occurred. It became the minority party in Congress until the 1994 mid-term elections and Newt Gingrich's 'Contract with America', which gave the GOP a majority in the House and Senate, lasting until 2006. The party was successful in winning presidential elections (with a 'southern strategy'), with Nixon winning in 1968 and 1972, Reagan in 1980 and 1984, George H. W. Bush in 1988 and George W. Bush in 2000 and 2004.

What does the Republican Party believe in?

The GOP is the more ideologically conservative party, with the following characteristics:

- It is committed to a free market economy as free as possible from government intervention and regulation, and supports a less active, more limited government role.

Knowledge check 20

What caused the rise of 'New Democrats' in the 1980s?

Examiner tip

Always distinguish between liberal, conservative and moderate Democrats, their views on issues, the kind of states and districts that they represent and how they vote in Congress.

Knowledge check 21

Explain the importance of the 'Contract with America' in 1994.

conservatism An ideological leaning on the right or centre right of the political spectrum. In the USA, conservatives were so called as they opposed the New Deal and today are more likely to accept the status quo without seeking to create artificial changes to society and its institutions through government intervention or regulation. There are several forms of conservatism including 'neo-conservatism', fiscal and social.

Knowledge check 22

Explain the different ideological views on the role of government held by Democrats and Republicans.

Examiner tip

Be very clear about the ideological views on economic, social and foreign policy that distinguish the Democratic Party from the Republican Party, and which also attract different types of voter to support them, showing synoptic links with voting behaviour explanations.

compassionate conservatism An attempt to marry 'Rockefeller Republican', socially liberal views with the fiscally conservative views of the Republican Party. It was associated with 'softer' views on education, immigration and welfare in George W. Bush's 2000 campaign. It is seen today in the views of the small 'rump' of moderate Republicans often labelled RINOs (Republicans in name only) by their more ideologically conservative fellow Republicans.

Examiner tip

Be able to distinguish between 'fiscal' and 'social' conservatives within the Republican Party and to give examples of the kind of issues that they support or oppose.

- It is fiscally conservative, committed to lower taxes, lower spending (with the exception of defence) and balanced budgets.
- It believes the private rather than the public sector should provide employment, health and welfare (although it supports Medicare, thought to be 'untouchable', because the elderly vote in large numbers).
- It does not support interventionist programmes to increase the rights of minority groups: its individualistic, self-help philosophy opposes the use of legislation as a way of 'artificially' creating equality.
- It is supportive of traditional family values and social and cultural conservatism.
- It is more hawkish on foreign policy issues, committed to high defence spending and the use of power to defend American interests.
- It is more committed to states' rights and the decentralisation of power.
- It takes a more 'pro-life' position on abortion and is against gun control, while supporting the death penalty and tougher immigration control.

As a result of these views and associated policies, the Republican Party has attracted voting support from:

- business and corporate interests
- higher-income voters
- white voters
- rural, small-town and suburban voters in the 'red' states
- religious groups, especially Protestants and evangelicals

What are the main divisions in the Republican Party?

Traditionally, the Republican Party was less factionalised than the Democrats, but during the Reagan presidency (1980–84 and 1984–88) ideological divisions grew between the more moderate and more conservative wings of the party:

- **The 'Wall Street' wing:** moderate, fiscally conservative but socially liberal Republicans, mainly from northeastern states, representing business and corporate interests. These are known as the 'Rockefeller Republicans' or **compassionate conservatives** of the party.
- **The 'Main Street' wing:** more conservative Republicans from rural, suburban and small-town America, supporting traditional family values and strongly anti-communist.

The 1980s saw the emergence of the **religious right**, radical right or New Right (neo-conservative) conviction-style politics associated with Reagan. The views of this increasingly significant faction in the party included:

- fiscal conservatism and strong commitment to small government, free markets and deregulation, expressed by Reagan's slogans: 'Government is the problem, not the solution' and 'Get government off the backs of the people'
- a more hawkish foreign policy and the 'Reagan Doctrine' of ultra anti-communism and high defence spending
- a much greater focus on social conservatism, with a religious agenda of opposition to abortion and support for school prayers and traditional family values

As a result, the party gained new support from:

- white voters in the South: since 1980 a majority of white southerners have identified and voted with the Republican Party

- the 'Reagan Democrats': the blue-collar, 'Joe Six-pack' workers in the northern industrial states who switched to the Republican Party because of its more conservative positions

With the support of this new 'Reagan Coalition' of voters, the Republican Party was successful in winning the presidency from 1980.

The 1994 'Contract with America' won the Republican Party a congressional majority with a highly conservative platform of ideas, which improved party cohesion in the House of Representatives in particular.

The party controversially won back the presidency in 2000, and won again in 2004, focusing on a socially conservative agenda based around the themes of 'Guns, Gays and God' and 'Faith, Flag and Family' as well as national security after 9/11. The conservative wing of the party has been ideologically dominant in Congress and the party base is highly conservative in its views. The Republicans' defeat in 2008 saw the demise of the formerly successful 'Reagan Coalition' and triggered a debate over the future direction of the party, with some fracturing along moderate and conservative ideological lines.

One key change has been the decline of the moderate/centrist faction of the Republican Party, with only a small 'rump' of moderate Republicans remaining, such as senators Susan Collins and Olympia Snowe of Maine and Lisa Murkowski of Alaska. They belong to the Main Street Partnership faction in Congress. These 'RINOS' are fiscally conservative but socially more liberal and do not always vote with their party in Congress. Their numbers have depleted because of defections to the Democrats, such as Arlen Specter's in 2009, electoral defeats or successful primary challenges because of their moderation.

Related to the decline of moderates in the Republican Party is the influence of the more fiscally conservative Tea Party movement since 2009, which has served to push the Republican Party further to the right and energised the conservative grass roots, fuelled by opposition to the bailouts and growing deficits in the economy. It had an impact on Republican turnout in 2010 and the Republican primaries. There is now a Tea Party caucus in the House with around 60 members led by Michelle Bachmann and a presence in the Senate with senators Rand Paul and Jim De Mint. However, while energising the base of conservative Republican voters, this may alienate more moderate, independent voters and has had little impact on the Democratic Party.

Internal coalitions

It is fair to say that both parties remain 'big tent' internal coalitions, although they are distinct from one another and more united internally on principles than they were in the past. Both parties contain a wide spectrum of ideological beliefs, and it is said that the labels 'Republican' and 'Democrat' are not accurate guides to the opinions of either voters or politicians: a prefix needs to be added, such as 'conservative', 'liberal' or 'moderate', to give the label meaning. Knowing the state, region or area that the voter or politician comes from can be a vital clue to their ideological convictions. There are economic conservatives and liberals, social conservatives and liberals, hawks and doves, isolationists and internationalists within each party.

religious right This socially conservative faction of Christian fundamentalists grew in opposition to the secularisation of the 1960s and 1970s, and particularly in reaction to the 1973 *Roe* v *Wade* decision on abortion. It now represents a large part of the base and core vote of the Republican Party. Sarah Palin was chosen as vice-presidential candidate by John McCain to boost his vote from these 'values voters' in 2008.

Examiner tip

Understand the impact that Reagan had on the Republican Party, changing its ideological direction and bringing electoral success.

Knowledge check 23

What has been the impact of the Tea Party movement on the Republican Party since 2008?

internal coalitions US parties are broad coalitions of interests and values with elected representatives having different views on political issues. There are wings and factions within each party, such as the Blue Dog Democrats and the Main Street Partnership in the Republican Party, each representing the views of liberals, moderates or conservatives within the 'big tent' US parties, making it difficult to hold to a 'party line'.

Party organisation

In comparison with their counterparts in the European democracies, where parties have strong, centralised structures, the two main US political parties are weaker, decentralised structures.

Constitutional context

The reason why US parties differ from their European counterparts in their organisation is linked to constitutional provisions:

- **The separation of powers.** The executive and legislature are separate branches of government, elected separately under different mandates and designed to check and balance each other's power. This impedes the development of strong party ties both within and between the institutions.
- **Federalism.** Under a federal system, parties are organised at state level, under state law, with little control by their national committees. This means that parties and their candidates differ widely across the 50 states. In this sense, there are effectively 50 Democratic and 50 Republican parties, with a 'bottom-up' rather than 'top-down' organisation.

What other factors lead to 'weak' parties in the USA?

- They have no mass membership (though voters can register as Democrat or Republican).
- There are no party leaders as such. The president is the leader of the country rather than of his party, and there is congressional leadership only through the speaker of the House and the Majority and Minority Leaders.
- There are no party manifestos, only 'platforms' decided at the conventions. Candidates for congressional and state office stand on their own personal views, and focus on local rather than national issues.
- The finance that candidates need in order to run for office is raised mainly by the candidates, not their parties.
- Candidates for office are selected by primaries and caucuses rather than by the party. They can only be removed by the electorate at the next election, or through primary defeat, and cannot be deselected by their parties.

The effect of the above factors is that there is little, if any, control by the parties over their candidates running for office, and so when individuals are elected to office they tend to vote the way that they want, not how the party tells them to. In Congress there is little party discipline to control their voting.

In electoral campaigns candidates rarely mention their party, but the key gift of the parties to their candidates is the party label, 'Democrat' or 'Republican'. This is the cue for aligned voters to turn out to vote for candidates with their preferred party label on the ticket.

Party decline and party renewal

Is the party over?

The debate over party decline started with David Broder's thesis in the 1970s that 'the party is over' because of the change to the parties' traditional functions.

There were five main arguments supporting the thesis.

Selection of candidates through primaries

Until the 1960s, parties selected candidates through machine politics and party bosses, but this changed with the use of primary elections, where candidates are chosen by voters, not by the party. Candidates now create personal organisations to appeal to voters and put across their personal views on issues. These intra-party contests weaken parties as candidates fight each other for nomination.

Changes to electoral finance

In most democracies, parties fund their candidates seeking election. In the USA, candidates raise 'hard money' contributions, gain funding from political action committees, or accept federal funding for presidential elections. This funding goes to the candidate, not the party, which reduces the party's organisational role in the campaign.

Changes in campaigning

Candidates now reach out to voters through the mass media and political advertising that focuses on the candidate and their image. Media campaigns strengthen candidate identification and weaken party identification, as they stress the characteristics of the candidate and play down the party. Victory is then seen as a personal, not a party, victory.

Growth of powerful interest groups and single-issue politics

US politics is now more characterised by pressure groups focusing on single issues such as abortion or the environment than by party politics.

Partisan de-alignment

Reduced attachment of voters to parties can lead to split-ticket voting, voters switching between parties, and higher abstention. Candidates make personal appeals to these independent voters to gain their votes.

However, most political commentators now write of the renewal and even resurgence of US parties, both ideologically and organisationally.

Examiner tip
The 'party's over' thesis is now outdated as, although US parties are still weak when compared to the centralised and disciplined UK parties, they are organisationally and ideologically stronger than when the journalist David Broder argued that they were in decline in 1971.

What is the evidence for ideological resurgence?

- The Republican Party is now more ideologically cohesive as a fiscally and socially conservative party. Karl Rove's strategy for Bush in 2004 and the impact of the Tea Party in 2010 were to energise the base of 'values voters' in order to get the core conservative voters out to the polls.
- The Democratic Party is now more ideologically cohesive and offers a clear alternative to the Republican Party, appealing to voters as a party of liberal values and policies, as seen in the 2008 campaign and support for healthcare reform, economic stimulus and banking regulation.
- Ideological cohesion is reflected in congressional voting, with greater party unity and increasing partisanship on issues. For example, Republicans were encouraged to vote together to support Bush's agenda after 2000, and the Democrats showed

Examiner tip

Have evidence of increasing party unity scores in congressional votes, showing greater partisanship and ideological polarisation. These can be found in *Congressional Quarterly*.

greater party unity in votes in the House of Representatives under the leadership of Nancy Pelosi. No Republican voted for healthcare reform (which they call 'Obamacare') in Congress in 2010.

What is the evidence for organisational resurgence?

While the parties are generally characterised by organisational weakness, several recent developments suggest that the national party structures may be playing a greater role:

- The parties' national committees and chairs are playing an increasingly important role between elections, as well as organising the national conventions every 4 years. This can be seen in the Brock reforms in the Republican Party and the Dean reforms for the Democrats.
- National party campaigning strategies have been created to elect the president and members of Congress and state legislatures, and these involve some party control over the direction and focus of the campaigns and how the parties' resources are targeted (e.g. the Democrats' 6 for 6 campaign in 2006).
- The role of the Democratic Party's super-delegates at the national convention could be important if there is a tie in the delegate count.
- The Democratic National Committee declined to seat the full Florida and Michigan delegations at the 2008 convention because of their refusal to follow party rules in conducting their state primaries.
- Both national committees now channel political donations to candidates in tight races and can withdraw finance from candidates they do not approve of.

US parties may be relatively weak in organisational terms, but there has been much evidence of party renewal and it may simply be the case that both parties have changed their role and functions rather than declined, and are simply different from what they were in the 1950s and 1960s. Rather than parties being 'over' we can conclude:

Examiner tip

Do not underestimate the changes that have taken place in the parties, both organisationally and ideologically in recent times, and be clear about the reasons for those changes.

- they are both still active at and between elections
- other parties have made no significant inroads into their support
- the majority of voters still identify with them
- it is very rare for any candidate to be elected without belonging to one or the other of them

The two-party system in the USA

Despite the USA's huge social, economic, regional and ethnic diversity, it has only two parties competing for political office at all levels in all branches of government. This duopoly has existed since the beginning of the Republic and is regarded as a paradox, since there are so many deep divisions in the population and only two parties to represent that huge diversity.

Why does the USA have a two-party system?

The electoral system and 'wasted votes'

In congressional elections, the use of the winner-takes-all system in single-member districts and states leads to two-party dominance, as votes for second and third parties are always wasted.

In presidential elections, voters vote for a single executive through the Electoral College. There can only be one winner, with no possibility of power-sharing in the presidency. There is nothing for the losers, no matter how many votes they gained.

'Catch-all' parties

The 'big tent' internal coalition nature of US parties and their habit of political 'clothes stealing', i.e. adopting popular policies put forward by their rivals, leaves little ideological or issue space for third parties to fill that is not already covered by the two main parties.

Partisan alignment

The party identification of most voters with the two parties is strong, and it is difficult to establish new alignments.

A natural duopoly

On most issues there are two opposing viewpoints: for or against, left or right, liberal or conservative, and therefore there is a tendency for voters to fall into one of two camps, Democrat or Republican.

Strong pressure groups

People focused on single issues tend to form pressure groups to get their views and interests represented, rather than establishing new parties to contest elections.

Primary elections

If individuals oppose what party candidates do they can challenge them in primaries. This gives voters a choice *within* the party, rather than requiring the formation of an alternative party.

Why are third parties not successful?

Apart from the strength of the two-party duopoly, third parties in the USA face additional difficulties.

Ballot access

Third parties face barriers in many states, such as electoral laws which require them to gather thousands of signatures before they can get onto the ballot.

Finance

Federal funding may be given to Democrats and Republicans, but other parties only get funding if they gained 5% of the vote at the previous election. It is difficult to secure alternative sources of finance, since organisations such as political action committees want to fund winners, not losers.

Campaigning

Lack of funding means less effective campaigns. Third-party candidates find it difficult to secure media attention and coverage of their issues, and consequently

Examiner tip
Make sure that you have examples of minor parties and independent candidates who have contested US elections and be able to show their actual or potential significance in those elections, and in US politics generally, using accurate evidence of their success or failure.

struggle to achieve name recognition or national awareness. They are usually excluded from the debates and lack electoral machines to persuade their supporters to turn out to vote.

Nevertheless, there have been some significant third parties and independent candidates in US elections. Some argue that Ralph Nader's candidacy in 2000, when he gained 2.7% of the vote, was a factor in Gore's defeat, as he took away votes in key states such as Florida, thus handing the election to Bush. Ross Perot's 19% of the vote in 1992 was a factor in George H. W. Bush's defeat, and his platform of deficit reduction influenced both parties to adopt this position in the 1996 election. George Wallace's 1968 candidacy, when he won 46 Electoral College votes from five southern states, could have deadlocked the Electoral College.

Most votes received by third parties are protest votes against the two main parties rather than positive votes for the third party concerned. It can be argued that despite their lack of electoral success, third parties have some importance within the electoral system, bringing new ideas on to the political agenda, acting as critics of the two main parties and offering a greater choice to voters.

However, none has come near to breaking the mould of American two-party politics or making an electoral breakthrough. They can never hold the balance of power or be part of a coalition, as the Liberal Democrats could in the UK Parliament. They are described as 'the bees of American politics', stinging briefly and then dying on the margin of the political system.

Finally, although the USA is described as having a two-party system, there are three factors that could be seen as bringing this into question in reality:

- There is effectively a four-party system, as both parties are divided into liberal and conservative wings.
- There is a 50- or 100-party system, with different Republican and Democratic parties in each of the 50 states.
- There are several one-party regions where one of the parties is dominant.

Knowledge check 25

Why are third parties referred to as 'the bees of American politics'?

Knowledge check 26

Give examples of one-party regions in the USA where one or other of the parties is dominant.

Comparison with UK parties

Political parties in the UK:

- have a mass membership
- have a centralised, top-down organisation
- select candidates for office at local level and can deselect MPs
- control the manifesto on which candidates for Parliament stand
- provide finance for, and direction of, the campaign
- select the leader, who becomes the prime minister or leader of the opposition, and can remove them by internal party procedures
- have strong party loyalty and party discipline through an effective whipping system

After studying this topic you should be able to:

- Identify the constitutional and historical factors that explain the nature of US parties.
- Identify and explain political liberalism in the USA and the main ideological views of the Democratic Party.
- Identify and explain political conservatism in the USA and the main ideological views of the Republican Party.
- Identify and explain the parties' main voting coalitions and bases of support, and any changes to these through realignments.
- Identify and explain the parties' internal divisions, giving examples of factions within each party.
- Show how and why US parties are described as organisationally weak.
- Explain the 'party decline' thesis of the 1970s.
- Explain using evidence and examples why parties are now more ideologically coherent and polarised.
- Explain using evidence and examples how parties have become organisationally stronger.
- Explain why the USA has such a strong two-party system in such a diverse nation.
- Identify and explain the difficulties facing third parties in breaking the two-party duopoly.
- Show how third parties may have some impact on the political and electoral systems despite these difficulties.
- Make relevant and appropriate references to UK parties to highlight differences.
- Understand the key debates surrounding the nature, roles, ideology and organisation of the two main parties, their similarities and differences, their decline and resurgence.
- Understand the debates concerning the role and significance of minor parties.

Voting behaviour

Voting behaviour in the USA is regarded as considerably more complex than in other democracies because of the variables involved and the fragmented and changing electorate to which the candidates have to appeal. Psephologists have developed various models of voting behaviour to analyse the factors influencing voters.

Partisan alignment — 1 lesson.

The **party identification** model stresses the importance of partisanship in explaining voting behaviour. Through long-term (primacy) factors such as family socialisation and socioeconomic status, individuals develop strong attachments to parties and align with those parties, not changing their vote from election to election, regardless of changing candidates and issues. These voters are the core voters or the base of the parties. Levels of partisanship fluctuate, but high levels lead to stable, fairly predictable patterns of voting behaviour.

Parties and their core voters

Voting behaviour is closely related to a voter's perception of his or her group interests and whether these are best represented by the Democrats or the Republicans. The two parties have attracted the support of diverse groups of voters, who perceive the party as representing their interests and reflecting their values. This relates to the history, ideology and policies of each party.

Examiner tip

Always refer to models of voting behaviour and concepts that psephologists have developed to analyse and explain the factors influencing the way people vote.

party identification

A strong psychological/ emotional attachment to parties gained through political socialisation which leads to habit voting regardless of candidates and issues. Such party loyalty is deep-rooted and resistant to change, leading to predictable and stable voting. Such partisanship can be weak or strong and may change in response to events such as white southern voters in the 1960s.

New Deal Coalition

Voting groups attracted to the Democrats by the 1930s New Deal reforms, alongside the white conservative voters in the 'solid' South whose alignment was a legacy of the Civil War. This new coalition of liberal groups and ethnic minorities in the North supporting the same party as the extremely conservative South collapsed when the Democrats adopted more liberal and civil rights platforms in the 1960s.

The Democratic Party

The Democratic Party is perceived as the more liberal party, associated with the less affluent and with minorities and offering interventionist policies to help them. Until the 1960s and the breakdown of the New Deal Coalition, it was also the party of the South. It is associated with more liberal positions on issues and policies, and therefore attracts more intellectual and progressive voters to its voting coalition.

The Republican Party

/ lesson.

The Republican Party is perceived as the more conservative party, associated with richer, WASP (White Anglo-Saxon Protestant) America, with policies favouring business, free markets and fiscal and social conservatism, and attracting more wealthy, white, rural and suburban voters to its voting coalition.

What social and economic factors influence voter choice?

Income

Although the social class factor is relatively insignificant in US political culture, there is a correlation between income levels and voting behaviour, with more affluent voters tending to vote Republican and the less affluent tending to support the Democrats. There are also occupational differences in voting: for example, unionised car workers are more likely to vote Democrat than business executives. This relates to the economic policies of the two parties.

Race and ethnicity

The USA has always been a melting pot of immigrant groups with different cultural identities and traditions. It has assimilated new immigrants, from the first WASP settlers, through waves of European immigration, and more recently to immigrants from Asia and Latin America.

The black vote

African-Americans have been the most overwhelmingly solid group of Democrat voters since the 1930s. At this time, the black vote, which had gone mainly to the Republicans since the days of Abraham Lincoln, realigned to support the Democrats in response to the policies of Franklin Roosevelt. Usually more than 90% of black voters vote Democrat at each election. The black vote is heavily concentrated in certain states and districts and in multi-ethnic cities.

Why is the black vote so heavily Democratic?

Many factors pull black voters towards the Democrats and push them away from the Republicans:

- The New Deal and Great Society legacy of activist government and welfare programmes, benefiting poorer groups of voters.
- The Democratic Party's support for the Civil Rights Movement and civil rights legislation.

- The Democrats' support for, and extension of, affirmative action programmes.
- Democratic black role models, including members of Congress, governors, mayors and the first black president.
- The Republican Party's failure to support or represent black interests and its image as the white party supported by white voters.

The last 50 years have seen increased mobilisation of the black vote, through the work of the National Association for the Advancement of Colored People (NAACP), Jesse Jackson's Rainbow Coalition and the Black Caucus in Congress. However, a problem for black voters has been that the Republican Party ignores them because it cannot win their vote and the Democratic Party takes them for granted because it can.

Republicans have tried to attract the votes of the black middle class through economic and socially conservative policies, appealing to richer or religious black voters, but with little success, as seen in the 95% vote for Obama in 2008.

The Hispanic vote

As a result of demographic change, with the Hispanic population the USA's fastest-growing minority, the Hispanic vote is now regarded as the sleeping giant of US politics. Hispanic voters are concentrated in several key districts and states with large Electoral College votes (e.g. Florida) and so are politically significant, with their votes sought by both parties. Most are Spanish speaking and over 70% are Roman Catholic, which has led to some vote switching from the Democrats to the Republicans over issues such as abortion. The majority, however, still vote Democrat for social rather than religious reasons, and many were mobilised to vote over the divisive issue of illegal immigration in 2008, when Obama won 66% of the Hispanic vote.

The Asian vote

The Asian population represents a growing group of voters not united by language or culture and having their origins in a number of countries, including Vietnam, Japan and Korea. In the 2004 election they voted 56% Democrat and 44% Republican.

Religion

The USA is unusual in that religious (and ethnic) identity has strongly influenced voting behaviour:

- The WASP vote was always strongly Republican because the early white settlers were Protestant.
- Catholic voters (of Irish and Italian descent as well as Hispanic) have historically identified with the Democratic Party as minorities. Some switched votes in 2004, attracted by the social conservatism of the Republicans on 'wedge' issues such as abortion and gay marriage, but they voted Democrat in larger numbers again in 2008.
- Jewish voters are traditionally Democrat because of their minority status and liberal views, are usually active in support of pro-Israel candidates and are a key voting bloc in New York and Florida.
- Christian fundamentalist voters are the cultural and social conservatives of US politics and strongly Republican, siding with religion in the so-called 'Culture Wars' against secular values. Religious cable channels offer voting guides and are strong in the Bible belt, the South, small towns and rural areas. Their influence on

Knowledge check 28

Why are both US parties reluctant campaigners for the black vote?

Knowledge check 29

Why are Hispanic voters increasingly targeted by the two parties in election campaigns?

Examiner tip

Be aware of the greater importance of religion and religious affiliation as a factor influencing voting behaviour in the USA compared to the UK.

gender gap This refers to the different voting patterns of men and women found in all modern elections, although the gap narrows or widens at each election as voters respond to different candidates and issues. Women voters are more likely to vote Democrat and men Republican. This links to the ideologies and policies of both parties being more or less attractive to the different genders.

the party may have served to alienate more moderate Republican voters who do not share their social conservatism. In 2004, one in four voters were evangelical Christians and almost 80% voted for Bush.

- All regular churchgoers are more likely to vote Republican, while secular voters are more likely to vote Democrat.

Gender

In elections, the Republican Party receives a majority of votes from men, and the Democratic Party a majority of votes from women, and more women than men turn out to vote. Recognition of the significance of the female vote was reflected in the attention given to 'security moms' in 2004 and 'hockey moms' in 2008 as important demographic groups of voters.

How can the 'gender gap' be explained?

Of course, apart from gender, all voters have other characteristics. Men and women may be rich or poor, black or white, liberal or conservative. However, the evidence suggests that women voters are more likely to vote Democrat because they:

- are more 'pro-choice' on abortion, more pro-gun control and anti-death penalty
- place more emphasis on health, education and welfare issues, and benefit from Democrat policies such as childcare
- dislike much Republican social conservatism and hawkish views on foreign policy, and place less emphasis on lower taxes than men
- are more environmentally aware, wanting more regulation

Age

Evidence is mixed, but there is little to show that age is a significant independent variable affecting voting behaviour. What can be said is that older voters are more likely to have a party identification and thus more likely to vote. This explains the emphasis both parties place on the 'grey vote' and issues that affect older voters, such as Medicare. Younger voters are more de-aligned and volatile, and not reliable voters, despite 'Rock the Vote' campaigns. In 2008 Obama won the votes of 68% of first-time voters, and 66% of the 18- to 29-year-old voters.

Region

Where a voter lives in the USA can be an important influence on their voting. This relates to the different social and economic characteristics of the states and areas within them. The southern states were solidly Democratic until the 1960s and have been solidly Republican since then. Voters in the rust belt, the industrial states, the coastal states and the cities ('blue America') are more likely to vote Democrat, and voters in the Bible belt, the mountain states and the rural and suburban areas within them are more likely to vote Republican ('red America').

US voters, therefore, have different group identifications and interests that influence the way they vote. If these reinforce one another, it is easier to predict voting behaviour. For example, a high-income, white, male, Protestant executive living in a Texas suburb is likely to be a reliable Republican voter, while a low-income, female, atheist, black waitress living in an inner city in Ohio is likely to be a Democrat.

Knowledge check 30

Why do parties focus on the 'grey vote' in US elections?

Examiner tip

Always use accurate statistical evidence from recent elections showing links between groups of voters with differing social and demographic characteristics and their support for the parties.

However, when there are cross-cutting identifications voting behaviour will be harder to predict.

Partisan de-alignment

An alternative model of voting behaviour stresses the increasing importance of short-term factors in explaining voting behaviour. The process of de-alignment sees voters losing, or having weaker, party attachments, and as a result they are more inclined to respond to specific candidates or issues than to vote on the basis of party loyalty.

Increased de-alignment leads, to a greater or lesser degree, to more volatility, a greater likelihood of ticket-splitting, increased numbers of **'swing' voters** and more abstention. It also means that parties must work harder to win votes, especially independents, as they can no longer rely on large numbers of core, aligned voters to always turn out and vote for them.

However, there are debates about the extent of de-alignment in the USA.

What are short-term (recency) factors influencing voting?

Candidate voting

De-aligned voters may vote differently in different elections because their voting is more influenced by the candidates (their personality, image, experience) than by their party allegiance. This is particularly the case in the age of media-dominated politics focusing on candidate-centred campaigns. A factor in George W. Bush's wins in 2000 and 2004 was that voters liked him more than they did Gore (seen as wooden) and Kerry (seen as elitist). Reagan's image was particularly important in his 1980 and 1984 wins. McCain may have been seen as too old and 'grumpy' in 2008 and Obama as the more impressive candidate.

Issue voting

De-aligned voters are also more likely to vote for candidates because of their views on specific issues, particularly in the age of single-issue politics, with economic issues usually being the most significant.

However, election issues change, and in 2004 it was said not to be 'the economy, stupid' (as in Clinton's 1992 campaign) but moral values that were uppermost when 'wedge issues' such as abortion and gay marriage were used to energise the base of the Republican Party to vote. Although moral issues have been important in influencing voters, there is evidence of a backlash against religious right values and they may now be vote-losers rather than winners. This seemed the case in 2008, when a severe economic crisis linked to the Republicans reduced prominence for moral issues in the campaign and a widespread sense among the electorate that it was 'time for change' helped to explain Obama's win and McCain's loss.

Performance voting

According to rational choice theories of voting behaviour, voters may vote on the performance or record of an incumbent or a future president. Retrospective voting suggests voters make judgements on past performance and vote against politicians with

---

Knowledge check 31

Give two examples of voters with 'cross-cutting identifications'.

'swing' voters Labelled floating in the UK and independent in the USA, swing voters are de-aligned and lack strong party identification, and their votes cannot be predicted or taken for granted. They are targeted in campaigns and can be crucial in deciding elections, especially in swing states. Approximately 30% of voters describe themselves as independent, although most 'lean' towards one party or another.

Knowledge check 32

Which issues were 'salient' at (a) the 2004 election, (b) the 2008 election?

Examiner tip

No two elections are the same. Be prepared to give evidence of different candidates, issues and events in several presidential elections producing different outcomes.

a poor performance in office, as in the case of Bush Senior in 1992 after recession, or they make a judgement on prospective performance, as with Obama in 2008. When voters are satisfied with his performance, the incumbent may be elected to a second term, as were Clinton in 1996 (economic boom) and George W. Bush in 2004 (war president). It is argued that voters are now more educated and informed on political issues and make rational choices according to the candidates, the issues they support and the events of the time.

A combination of several factors is at work in each election, as voters react to different candidates, salient issues and events. Rarely do candidates appeal to party loyalty, as they know they must reach out to influence the independent 'swing' voters and those with a weak party identification in order to win.

What is 'split-ticket' voting?

Because of the separation of powers and federalism, US voters face a choice from a range of candidates, for several offices, on the same ballot paper on the same day. Voters can vote the 'straight ticket' by voting for the same party for each office. Voters who vote for candidates for office from different parties on the same ballot paper at the same election are 'splitting their ticket'. The simplest reason why voters do this (although it may seem irrational) is because they can. Other reasons include voter **de-alignment** and the influence of different candidates and issues, so voters are making complex choices by voting for different parties for different reasons.

Split-ticket voting was high in the 1970s and 1980s, and in 1984 55% of Democratic identifiers voted for Reagan, but he was faced with a Democrat majority in the House. However, split-ticket voting has fluctuated in recent elections.

The main consequence of split-ticket voting is divided government in Washington, leading to the much-criticised legislative 'gridlock'. However, the outcome of split-ticket voting may be positive for voters, as it can mean they get the best of both worlds through their votes: for example, voting for a Republican president can mean low taxes but strong defence and voting for a Democrat member of Congress can mean higher spending on welfare. Split-ticket voting also helps to prevent 'elective dictatorship', since the voters' choices result in more effective checks and balances.

Abstention in US elections

It is paradoxical that in the country that is the world's greatest advocate of democracy, turnout at elections is among the lowest in the democratic world, particularly as other forms of participation, such as pressure group activity, are high. It is important, however, to note the distinction between figures for the turnout of the voting age population, which includes all voters over 18 whether registered or not, non-citizens and felons, and those for the turnout of registered voters. When measured by voting age population, turnout appears low, whereas there is usually a high turnout of registered voters.

How can high abstention be explained?

Voter registration

In most states, voters have to make some effort to get registered, but it is now easier, as the Help America Vote Act 2002 allows same-day registration and early voting

---

de-alignment This term refers to the lack or loss of party identification, so it links with the concept of independent swing voters. De-aligned voters lack or lose partisan loyalty gained through socialisation into party identification from an early age. De-alignment links with volatility, split-ticket voting and higher abstention, as well as candidate and issue voting. Younger voters are more de-aligned than older voters.

split-ticket voting Federalism and the separation of powers enable voters to vote for different parties on the same ballot in the same election on the same day. Voters who vote for different parties for whatever reason (candidates/issues) are voting a split rather than a straight party ticket, and can be seen by examining voting statistics in states showing different levels of support for different candidates from the same party.

Knowledge check 33

Explain the difference between the voting age population and the voting eligible population.

---

in many states. There are registration drives to mobilise the vote and there are no barriers to voting (except for felony in some states). Despite this, many voters fail to register. The registration process does not fully explain why voters do not register and why registered voters do not turn out to vote, so other explanations are needed:

'Democratic overload' and 'voter fatigue'

The huge number of elections for a wide range of posts from the president down to local civic officials and the resulting sense of permanent campaigning cause voters to switch off.

Media-dominated campaigns

The politics of soundbites, photo-opportunities and negative advertising, with candidates spending millions of dollars to say little about real issues, can alienate voters.

Lack of choice

Candidates may fail to impress voters, as in the 2000 campaign, characterised as 'Bore v Gush', and in that of 2004, described as the Texas cowboy against the Boston elitist. Parties may be perceived as uninspiring, failing to offer a clear choice of values and principles.

Decline in partisanship

Voters with strong party identification use their vote, while those without tend not to. When the numbers in the latter category increase, turnout falls.

The electoral system and the Electoral College

In 'safe' states and districts many people see little point voting: if a voter's preferred candidate has so little support that they cannot win (or so much that they cannot lose), there is little incentive to vote.

Voter apathy and cynicism

Some voters feel that voting does not make any difference to their lives, and that remote, lobbyist-dominated government in Washington is not responsive to their views. Cynicism has been increased by dissatisfaction with presidential performance and political scandals.

'Hapathy'

The idea that voters are so content that they do not need to vote is known as 'hapathy'. In this view, it is satisfaction with the system, not alienation from it, that reduces turnout.

Turnout fluctuates in each election; in 2008 it rose to 64%, the highest since 1960, with 131 million voters casting ballots. One reason for this was the success of the 'Ground War' turn-out-the-vote effort, while other significant factors were the important issues surrounding the election, the availability of more inspiring candidates and the absence of widespread negative campaigning.

democratic overload
Federalism and the separation of powers mean that there are numerous elections at different levels of government and for different offices as well as primaries and direct democracy. Americans vote 'for the president to the local dog-catcher' in 80,000 units of government, leading to 'permanent' campaigns and 'bed-sheet ballots' which may lead to voter fatigue, higher alienation levels and abstention through too many participation opportunities.

Examiner tip
The causes of relatively high US abstention levels are explained by multiple factors relating to the electoral and political systems. It is never enough to state that voters are simply 'bored' or 'apathetic' or 'cynical'. Boredom, apathy or cynicism must be explained.

Knowledge check 34
Why does turnout fluctuate in presidential elections?

differential abstention
Voters vote or abstain differently at each election, which may be won or lost according to which voters turn out to vote and which do not. Large numbers of young and minority voters voted for Obama in 2008, but failed to vote in the 2010 mid-term elections, while many Republican voters who abstained in 2008 voted in the 2010 mid-terms, giving the Republican Party success.

Examiner tip
Statistical and demographic information relating to US voting behaviour can be obtained through the Pew Research Centre (www.pewresearch.org) and the US Census Bureau (www.census.gov).

Differential abstention

Elections can be decided by who turns out to vote and who doesn't and this is different in each election. One in every three voters who voted in 2008 did not vote in 2010, as a result of an 'enthusiasm gap'.

More low-income, less educated, younger and minority voters tend to abstain, which damages the Democrats' prospects. Abstention is lower among high-income, elderly, educated, suburban white voters, which helps the Republican cause.

Turnout is lower in the mid-terms, where incumbency may be a strong factor influencing outcomes, and is even lower for primary elections.

Low turnout undermines the winning candidates' claim to mandates and legitimacy, and is regarded as a flaw in a representative democracy.

Some comparisons with the UK

Voting behaviour in the UK (in comparison with the USA) is characterised by:

- easy and compulsory registration of voters
- high turnout (although not in 2001, when turnout dropped to 59%)
- the requirement for the voter to mark the ballot paper with a single cross: ticket splitting is not possible
- fewer voting opportunities
- the role of class as the single most important determinant of the vote
- less emphasis on religious or ethnic factors influencing voting behaviour

Summary

After studying this topic you should be able to:

- Understand and use key psephological concepts and models of voting behaviour.
- Understand and explain the broad voting coalitions supporting each of the two parties, their core voting support and any changes that have taken place to these.
- Know that the outcomes of US elections are affected by a mixture of long-term and short-term factors affecting the way voters vote and that these are different at each election.
- Understand and explain the links between the social characteristics of US voters (socioeconomic status, gender, religion, race and ethnicity, age and region) and their support for the parties.

- Explain the importance of recency factors affecting the outcome of each election, such as different candidates, issues and events influencing voting behaviour.
- Understand the causes and the consequences of split-ticket voting in US elections.
- Understand the causes and consequences of differing levels of abstention at each US election.
- Make comparisons with voting in the UK where relevant and appropriate.
- Recognise the key debates and competing arguments in the study of US voting behaviour.

Pressure groups

What is a pressure group?

Pressure groups are organised groups of people who share a common interest that they wish to protect or a common aim that they wish to promote. They seek to influence public policy by gaining access to decision makers who have power. Therefore, compared to parties, pressure groups represent narrower interests and have narrower aims, do not put up candidates in elections and do not seek or take responsibility for government.

Pressure groups are found in a pluralist democracy where citizens can form or join groups to express their very diverse views and interests to government. **Pluralist** theory is associated with the political scientist Robert Dahl, who argued that governments respond to citizens' views expressed through competing pressure groups which all have the potential to influence decision making.

Pluralists take a positive view of pressure groups and argue that as a result of their activities political power is dispersed within the political system, although they do not consider that all pressure groups have an equal influence on government. Pluralists argue that groups are only influential in narrow policy areas: for instance, the American Medical Association (AMA) has influence on health policy but not on foreign policy. Also, on most issues there are *countervailing groups*: for example, 'pro-choice' groups promote a different agenda from 'pro-life' groups.

This pluralist view of pressure groups, however, is challenged by proponents of **elite theory**, who argue that power is not dispersed but is in fact highly concentrated, with some groups much more powerfully organised to influence the political agenda. They argue that there is not a level playing field when it comes to influence over political decisions.

In a pluralist democracy, thousands of groups form in order to try to influence government. This means that some classification of pressure groups is necessary, to distinguish between them and what they do.

What are the main types of pressure group in the USA?

Economic pressure groups

Business groups can gain access to, and influence over, economic decision making and include multi-national corporations such as Microsoft, and 'peak' associations speaking for the business community, such as the US Chamber of Commerce. Labour groups are trade unions which are active on issues affecting their members' interests. The 'peak' association speaking for this sector is the AFL/CIO, which lobbies on behalf of organised labour. It usually supports the Democratic Party, providing funds and campaign workers. Professional associations are 'protective' groups organised to defend specific occupational interests, such as the AMA, which represents US doctors and has been active in opposing attempts to expand universal healthcare.

Examiner tip
Make sure you have a clear understanding of what pressure groups are, why they form and how they differ from political parties.

pluralism A theoretical perspective on pressure groups which emphasises that groups are free to form and lobby, and that power is broadly, though unequally, dispersed among groups competing to influence public policy. Pluralism stresses the diversity of pressure groups, competition between them and dispersal of political power and influence within the open, fragmented political system, allowing all interests to be heard and represented.

Knowledge check 35

What is meant by countervailing groups? Give two examples.

elite theory Elite theorists argue that pressure group power is concentrated (not dispersed, as in the pluralist model) and that financially privileged groups such as business and corporate groups that represent the wealthy and powerful wish to preserve their vested interests. They have greater resources for lobbying, electioneering and access, and therefore exercise a disproportionate influence on policy decisions. They are the power elite.

Single-issue lobbies

In recent years there has been a huge growth in the number of groups representing single issues and specific causes. Examples include 'pro-choice' and 'pro-life' groups on the issue of abortion and the NAACP on the issue of civil rights.

Public interest lobbies

Consumer groups and citizens' lobbies, seeking a more collective good, have grown as new public interest issues and 'causes' have surfaced, such as the Sierra Club, an environmental group lobbying on environmental issues, and the American Civil Liberties Union (ACLU), formed to promote and protect citizens' liberties. Common Cause, a public interest group, puts the case for consumer rights and has battled against the corporate oil and tobacco lobbies in the USA.

Why has activity grown in recent years?

- The growth of government intervention in health, welfare and the environment means that government regulates large areas of citizens' lives, so groups are formed to defend their interests vis-à-vis government.
- A highly specialised and socially diverse society like the USA has thousands of different occupations and views on issues, with groups forming to protect and promote these.
- The complexity of modern government decision making means that lobbying is needed to provide specialised information to decision makers.
- One of the shortcomings of representative democracy expressed through voting at elections is that a 'blanket vote' for party candidates means citizens cannot express their specific views and interests.
- There is widespread recognition that individuals have little effect politically: only when organised can they have an impact on government.

It is said that the growing number of lobbies operating in US politics leads to a state of 'hyper-pluralism', in which government is overloaded with demands from powerful groups.

How do they achieve their aims?

Pressure groups in the USA use different methods at different times. Their success in achieving their aims depends on a number of important variables:

- **The structure of the political system.** This is highly fragmented, through the separation of powers and federalism, into numerous access points for group influence.
- **The nature of the party system.** Political parties are relatively weak organisations.
- **The political culture/values.** US political culture is based on openness and a strong awareness of constitutional rights, such as 1st Amendment rights of freedom of speech and assembly, and the 2nd Amendment's right to bear arms.
- **The issue the group is concerned with.** This may be a foreign, social, economic, environmental or moral issue, and it may be popular or unpopular.
- **The party in power.** Democrats are more sympathetic to groups supporting liberal or minority issues, and Republicans are more sympathetic to the views of business and religious groups.

- **The aims of the group.** A group pressing for more rights for war veterans is more likely to get public support and a sympathetic hearing than one concerned with the rights of prisoners.

Access points in the political system

This relates to the points where pressure groups can gain access to government in order to influence decisions. The US system of government is fragmented, open and multi-access. It is important to note that a group cannot influence anyone until it has access to them and their decision making.

The legislative branch

The House of Representatives and the Senate are equally powerful houses. Party allegiance has a relatively weak influence on the way members of Congress vote, so both houses are open to influence from pressure groups, especially if the group in question helped fund a member's campaign. Because Congress has a fragmented power structure of committees and sub-committees, some pressure groups can gain access here, where they focus on lobbying on the detail of legislation passing through both houses.

The executive branch

This branch of government may be lobbied via the Executive Office of the President (EXOP) or through access to federal government departments and agencies where policy or legislation originates or is implemented. The president also has the power of veto over legislation, and pressure groups may lobby for this to be used if they have failed to halt a bill they dislike in either house of Congress.

The judicial branch

The Supreme Court makes crucial decisions on controversial issues, so some pressure groups try to exert influence here:

- The NAACP uses the Supreme Court to challenge segregation by providing amicus curiae (friend of the court) briefs to influence its decisions and the NRA was involved in the landmark case *DC* v *Heller* in 2009, supporting 2nd Amendment rights.
- The American Civil Liberties Union (ACLU) brings test cases before the court, dealing with issues such as imprisonment without trial in Guantanamo Bay.
- Pressure groups may try to influence presidential selection of Supreme Court justices when a vacancy arises, or in Senate confirmation hearings.

This federal separation of powers is mirrored at the state level of government. Many decisions affecting groups are made at the state level, so pressure groups lobby here: for example, influencing state laws relating to abortion and its accessibility.

What are the most important factors affecting the success of pressure groups?

To succeed in gaining access to decision makers, pressure groups need a range of resources. These will vary, but they include the following.

Knowledge check 37

Which pressure groups are more likely to support and gain support from (a) the Democratic Party, (b) the Republican Party?

Knowledge check 38

Why and how is the Supreme Court used as an access point by some pressure groups?

Membership

- A large membership is especially important when supporters of the pressure group are likely to vote. The American Association of Retired People (AARP), for example, speaks on behalf of 40 million members.
- A small but powerful and active membership can also be very effective, such as the National Rifle Association (NRA), with over 4 million members.
- A dispersed membership can make up an important voting bloc in all the states: this is true, for example, of the Veterans.

Money

Groups raise money to try to gain access to elected politicians through financial contributions to their campaigns, either through political action committee money (see later) or by 'spending on behalf of' candidates, buying advertising to promote issues that may help their favoured candidates to win.

Professional lobbyists

Wealthy pressure groups hire professional **lobbyists** to make links with members of Congress in order to try to influence their voting in committees where the details of legislation are worked out. Especially important are former members of Congress, who may pass through the 'revolving door' widely perceived as linking service in Congress with jobs in the lobbying sector, and be hired by groups wishing to use their expert knowledge of Capitol Hill and their contacts there to influence decisions.

Information and expertise

Because the majority of political issues are now highly complex and technical, some pressure groups will gain access to congressional decision making because they have the specialist knowledge needed to testify in congressional hearings.

Other factors

- Groups are more influential when united in their aims, and weaken when they are internally divided.
- Groups are more effective when they are concerned with narrow policy aims or issues accepted by public opinion as realistic and worth supporting.
- Groups are more effective when they are inside government decision making. The strong relationship between powerful groups and government (known as 'clientelism') is referred to as an **iron triangle**, linking a pressure group, a federal government department or agency and the relevant congressional committee in a relationship which is hard to break or regulate.

What 'outsider' strategies are pursued by US pressure groups?

Many pressure groups in the USA lack the resources described above, and so fail to gain access. Others do not wish to pursue an insider strategy. In both cases, they use different methods of influence to achieve their aims:

- **Public campaigns.** Groups try to influence public opinion through the media in order to exert an indirect influence on politicians, in the knowledge that most politicians pay attention to the views of 'the folks back home' in their districts and states, particularly near election time.
- **Grass-roots lobbying and mass mailing campaigns.** These have become more important as electronic technology progresses, allowing groups to mobilise supporters to swamp their representatives with e-mail or letters in an attempt to influence their votes. They may publish ratings on voting records relating to the group's aims.
- **Direct action and demonstrations.** Because of 1st Amendment rights, taking to the streets as a form of protest is common in the USA. The aim is to draw media, public and congressional attention to the group and its aims, to raise public awareness and show strength of feeling on the issue. Examples include the Civil Rights campaigns of the 1950s and 1960s, anti-war demonstrations, the Million Mom March in 2000 over guns and the Occupy Wall Street anti-capitalist protest of 2011.
- **The initiative process.** Grass-roots activity is particularly important in states that allow initiatives. Pressure groups raise signatures to initiate a proposition on the ballot paper supporting their aims. They then campaign for this to be passed at state level.

direct action Groups with little or no access to decision makers may use 'outsider' strategies to influence them indirectly by gaining media and public attention. Direct action may be violent or illegal, such as actions to close down abortion clinics, or non-violent, such as demonstrations and forms of Civil disobedience seen during the Civil Rights Movement. This may reflect weakness rather than strength.

Some pressure groups are very successful in achieving their aims and others are not. Some get what they want most of the time, but others do not. It all depends on variables.

Are pressure groups a threat to democracy?

Those who believe that pressure groups are inevitable in a liberal, pluralist democracy and beneficial to it argue that they are *not* a threat to democracy:

- Pressure groups are the voice of the people, representing specific views and interests not catered for by catch-all parties and 'blanket votes' at elections.
- They encourage citizens' participation and involvement in politics.
- They link citizens and government between elections, keeping governments aware of different views on issues.
- The competing views of pressure groups help governments to decide where the public interest lies on issues such as environmental protection.
- Pressure group balance means that on most issues there are competing voices, such as business and labour.
- Groups play a valuable role in governmental decision making, in that they provide the expertise, cooperation and consent needed if policy is to work.

Others believe that pressure groups are too powerful and hinder the workings of a liberal democracy, and thus *are* a threat to it:

- There is unequal representation of interests, with many groups lacking access to the corridors of power or the resources to acquire it.
- Some interest groups are unorganised or ineffectively organised (e.g. the poor, who can be ignored), while others are powerfully organised (e.g. corporate lobbies such as energy companies, which are always consulted).

Examiner tip

Different pressure groups use different methods at different times and with different degrees of success, so make sure you can give examples of these variables and be careful not to over-generalise when analysing their activities.

Examiner tip

There are debates, but no agreement, on whether pressure groups enhance democracy or hinder it, so be aware of the arguments used on both sides of the analysis.

- Some single-issue groups threaten the democratic process by blocking reforms in areas such as gun law reform (NRA) or environmental regulation (oil and energy lobbies) which are wanted by a majority of the population.
- Budget deficits are linked to strong lobbies pressing for more resources and too strong to be denied by members of Congress seeking re-election.
- There is criticism of methods used by some groups, such as the role of political action committees in electoral finance or 'pro-life' groups harassing workers in abortion clinics.

Are there checks to pressure group power?

- The number of access points means groups may get what they want in the House but not in the Senate, or may achieve their aims at federal but not state level. Access does not mean success.
- The variety of pressure groups and countervailing groups creates a degree of balance.
- The Federal Election Campaign Act (FECA) places restrictions on political action committees' funding of candidates that must be disclosed.
- The mass media, protected by 1st Amendment rights, may uncover lobbying scandals, such as the Jack Abramoff 'influence peddling' case in 2006.
- Public opinion can restrain pressure group power, as members of Congress listen to 'the folks back home' even when being swamped by an artificially manufactured 'astro-turf' pressure group mail campaign.
- Legal restrictions on lobbying make it illegal to offer bribes to members of Congress, and all lobbyists must register as such, making their activities open and transparent.
- The Honest Leadership and Open Government Act of 2007, passed as a result of the Abramoff case, led to the tightening of regulations on lobbying activities such as a 2-year 'cooling off' period and the banning of gifts and sponsored trips for members of Congress.

The answer to the question of whether pressure groups are too powerful is 'It depends.' No pressure group is all-powerful.

Examiner tip

Do not underestimate the significance of checks to pressure group power and the constraints on their activities in a democracy. The Centre for Responsive Politics website (www.opensecrets.org) tracks pressure group activities and funding.

Political action committees

Political action committees (PACs) are the financial arms of pressure groups, set up to raise campaign funds and channel them to support or oppose candidates in electoral contests. They grew after the FECA reforms of the 1970s restricted fund-raising from organisations and 'fat cats', leaving a funding gap to be filled. They are limited in the amount of hard money they can donate to candidates ($5,000), but they 'bundle' these contributions to increase the sum given. They also give money for 'issue advocacy' to advertise 'on behalf of' candidates. Most PACs are pragmatic in their support, donating to candidates from both parties who will win, which generally means incumbents rather than challengers. This helps them achieve access to decision makers, especially the chairs and members of congressional committees affecting their interests. The role of PACs is controversial, with debates over their effect on US politics:

- Their impact on the electoral process, with millions of dollars raised and spent by groups, can be vital in a close race. Some argue that members of Congress will not speak out against powerful interests (e.g. the NRA or the pro-Israel lobby) because they are afraid of being targeted for defeat.

- They bolster the rise of candidate-centred campaigns, as they support candidates, not parties. Elected candidates then feel more beholden to them than to their parties, which can affect congressional voting.
- They encourage influence peddling in a 'coin-operated Congress' where it is alleged you 'have to pay to play'.
- They can deter challengers to incumbent members of Congress.
- New Super PACS emerged after the *FEC* v *Citizens United* case in 2010, allowing the unlimited raising and spending of campaign funds as long as they do not coordinate their activities with the parties or candidates (see p. 17).

(see p. 17)

Knowledge check 41

Why are political action committees and their activities often criticised?

Comparisons with UK pressure groups

- The UK offers fewer access points, as it has a fusion of power and a unitary system.
- There are fewer checks and balances in the UK, so less opportunity for groups to influence and block legislation.
- The UK has a strong party system, so MPs are protected from group influence by a strong party line.
- UK candidates are funded by the parties, not pressure groups with PACs.
- There are no entrenched rights and less open government in the UK, so group activity is less effective.
- There are fewer opportunities for US-style groups to operate in the UK, with no primaries and no initiatives.
- There is a clearer distinction in the UK between 'insider' groups that have access to Whitehall and 'outsider' groups that do not.

Summary

After studying this topic you should be able to:

- Define pressure groups and show how and why they arise in a representative democracy.
- Show that there are different theoretical perspectives on the role of pressure groups in a representative democracy.
- Give examples of different types of pressure group operating in the US political system.
- Show why pressure groups and their activities have grown in recent years and why US political culture encourages this activity.
- Give examples of the variables that affect the methods that pressure groups use to try and achieve their aims and objectives.
- Explain the different access points that pressure groups may use to further their specific aims and why different groups may use different access points at different times.
- Explain the reasons why some pressure groups may be more successful than others in achieving their aims.

- Explain, using examples, why some pressure groups may resort to 'outsider' strategies to try and achieve their aims.
- Evaluate the ways in which pressure group activity may enhance representative democracy.
- Evaluate the criticisms made of some pressure group activities and methods that may serve to hinder the workings of representative democracy.
- Know of the several checks to pressure group power in the USA, including legislative ones, and that not all groups are all-powerful all of the time.
- Evaluate the causes and the consequences of the growth of political action committees in campaign finance.
- Make comparisons where relevant and necessary to the relatively weaker pressure groups that operate in the UK political system.
- Recognise the key debates and competing arguments on the role and influence of pressure groups in the US political system.

Questions & Answers

This section looks at answers to examination questions on Unit 3A and follows the four areas previously identified in the specification.

The unit test explained

The Unit 3A exam is 90 minutes in length and you must answer two questions from a choice of four. The questions will reflect the four parts of the unit.

Each of the four questions has two parts:

- Part (a) is worth 10 marks and is a short-answer question. This should be completed in around 8–10 minutes. If you spend more time on this, you will eat into the time needed to complete the more mark-rich and challenging essays.
- Part (b) is worth 30 marks and is an extended essay. At least 30–35 minutes should be spent on each of the two essays chosen.

The two parts will be connected in the sense that they are part of the same topic area being assessed. They are not necessarily connected in any other way, to prevent any possible overlap in the answers given to both questions.

Assessment objectives at A2

Although the three assessment objectives at A2 are the same as at AS, they are weighted differently. At A2 more marks are awarded for analysis (AO2) than for knowledge (AO1).

AO1: Demonstrate knowledge and understanding of relevant institutions, processes, political concepts, theories and debates.

AO2: Analyse and evaluate political information, arguments and explanations, and identify parallels, connections, similarities and differences between aspects of the political systems studied.

AO3: Construct and communicate coherent arguments, making use of a range of appropriate political vocabulary.

When you write your answer both to part (a) and part (b), you will be given marks for all three of these assessment objectives. These will be totalled to give the mark for each part of the question, with a maximum score of 40 (10 + 30) for each question. The total mark for the unit is 80. This means that the total mark can be achieved in a variety of ways, and students may show different strengths or weaknesses in their answers. Generally, a very good student will achieve high marks on all three assessment objectives, as the answer will demonstrate high levels of knowledge and understanding and excellent analytical skills, will have structure and coherence, and will include impressive political vocabulary. However, it is possible to gain high marks for one objective and lower marks for another. For example, a student's knowledge of a topic may be impressive but the answer may lack focus and analysis and it may not be very clearly communicated. This means the mark may be high on AO1 but lower on AO2 and AO3. You should be aware of these assessment objectives and practise them throughout the year in homework essays and timed essays in class.

Levels of response

A2 assessment uses a generic mark scheme including levels of response, which examiners follow in order to allocate marks to students' answers. There is also a separate mark scheme for each specific question, reflecting the content expected in the answer.

- Level 4 is the highest level of response. Students who achieve marks at the top of this level will have written answers which are comprehensive, fully address the requirements of the question, give clear and accurate evidence and excellent examples and include developed theories and concepts, communicating clearly and effectively with focus, direction and conclusions. These are high A students.
- Level 3 responses are 'good' rather than 'excellent'. Students 'clearly' rather than 'comprehensively' address the requirements of the question and give 'good' evidence and examples, communicated 'well'.
- Level 2 responses are characterised by the key word 'limited', where students show limited knowledge, with a limited attempt to address the requirements of the question, limited evidence, examples and concepts, and communication which is limited in clarity, vocabulary, focus and direction.
- Level 1 responses should be avoided at all costs. At the bottom of this level it is barely worth entering the examination room. The key word here is 'little': the student shows little in terms of knowledge, focus, evidence, examples and clear communication. These responses are usually simplistic or superficial narrative with little clarity.

On the following pages, each sample question is accompanied by two answers written under timed conditions. One is of A-grade standard and the other of C-grade standard. None of the answers should be regarded as a perfect response. Each answer featured here only represents a way of approaching the question set, followed by an indication of the grade that it is likely to achieve and why.

After each of the questions, there is a section indicated by ⊜ identifying the focus of the question and what is expected in the answer. Each answer is followed by an 'examiner's comment' indicated by the symbol ⊜: this section comments on the approach of the answer and explains some of the reasons why it has achieved the grade indicated or how a higher mark could have been achieved. If you read these sections carefully, you will get an idea of how to improve your mark in the real examination for both parts of the question. It will also help you become more familiar with the assessment objectives.

It would be good practice to attempt your own answers *before* looking at the student answers and the comments made, so that you can do your own comparisons and make any adjustments likely to increase your mark.

It is important to note that this section does not offer any 'model answers' that can be reproduced in an examination. Most examination questions are worded differently, even when they are in the same specification area, and it is possible to achieve exactly the same grade for a question in different ways, by scoring on the assessment objectives with different strengths, weaknesses, evidence and examples. At A2, remember that not just knowledge and description (AO1) but also the higher-level skills of analysis and evaluation (AO2) are especially important if you are to gain higher marks.

How to achieve top grades

- Make sure you have covered all the specification topics in your revision to extend your question choice and to understand links between the four areas of GOV 3A.
- Consult mark schemes and assessment objectives to understand how examiners will mark your answers.
- Answer the question that has been set, not the one you wish had been set.
- Analyse the question. Identify key words in the question and refer to them in your answer where possible. Make a short plan that will guide your answer.
- Always keep a tight focus on the question asked, in the introduction, in the middle and at the end. Don't drift from its key demands.
- Use up-to-date examples and evidence to back up your arguments at all times.
- Show contextual awareness and understanding of the topic wherever possible.
- Use political concepts, theories and vocabulary, quoting political scientists or political thinkers if possible.
- Avoid learnt model answers based on questions set in previous papers.
- Use your time well: don't repeat points already made, and don't conclude your answer by simply repeating all you have said before.
- Avoid simplistic assertions and sweeping generalisations in your answers. Don't give your personal opinions or use the word 'I'.
- Be aware of debates surrounding political topics. The answer to many political questions is 'It depends', and valid (although not necessarily equal) arguments can be identified on both sides of any political debate.
- Make sure you use a good writing style, usually determined by lots of essay-writing practice throughout the year. Write with clarity and direction, with good grammar, vocabulary, spelling and legibility, to make a good overall impression on the examiner, who is going to give you a mark for your communication skills. Essays that gain high marks will have a good introduction setting the essay in context, well-developed and convincing arguments backed up by evidence and examples wherever possible, and a conclusion that draws the threads together. Lack of coherence substantially reduces marks.
- Although there are times when a passing reference to your UK politics course will be relevant to demonstrate synoptic understanding, especially of differences between the politics of the two countries, do not feel that artificial UK references have to be added to every point made or simply add on a reference to the UK at the end of the essay almost as an afterthought. Synoptic understanding demonstrates understanding of the A-level course as a whole, not just its parts, and the links both within and between the modules.
- Students who enter the examination room unprepared and lacking in serious study, and whose answers are unfocused, confused and poorly written, with little evidence of knowledge, understanding and analytical and communication skills, are unlikely to achieve the grade they wish for — but they may get the grade they deserve.

Question 1 Electoral process and direct democracy

(a) Explain the differences between caucuses and primaries in the presidential nomination process.
(10 marks)

ⓔ When answering this question it is essential to focus on explaining differences between the two selection methods in the nomination process rather than simply describing what each does, although it is necessary to demonstrate some knowledge (AO1) of how each works in selecting the party's nominee. You should give examples of both primaries and caucuses. For higher marks, you need to provide some analysis (AO2) of factors such as the different types of voter involved, the different degrees of democratic choice and the likely different outcomes.

A-grade answer

(a) Both primaries and caucuses are held to select the presidential candidate of each party, with the electorate voting in 'open' or 'closed' primaries **c**. They both occur on a state-wide basis and are held under state law **a**. They allow serious presidential candidates to present themselves, demonstrating that they wish to be the president in the coming election. Open primaries are those in which any registered voter can take part, even if from a different political party, whereas in closed primaries only registered voters of a specific party can take part **d**. Primaries and caucuses have essentially the same role, determining who will be a presidential candidate at the national conventions through the selection of delegates **a**. One difference is that caucuses are not open to the public, because only party activists vote, and therefore they are less democratic than primaries in the way presidential candidates are chosen **b**. They are associated with old-style, undemocratic 'machine politics' **c** and are found in the states with smaller populations **a**. Primaries and caucuses take place when the specific state requires them, but there has recently been a trend towards 'front-loading' **c** with some states holding their primary or caucus early on, believing it adds emphasis to the candidates they favour. However, the New Hampshire primary and the Iowa caucus are always the first and arguably the most important, as both show the first signs of who the electorate will support **a**. Many argue, though, that the low turnout at both primaries and caucuses leads to unrepresentative results **b**.

ⓔ **a** This answer demonstrates good (AO1) knowledge of both primaries and caucuses, but as well as describing them, **d** the student could have focused more on explaining differences between them (AO2) for a top Level 4 mark rather than wasting time on explaining the different kinds of primaries. **b** Although there is some AO2 analysis of the two ways of choosing party candidates, the answer could have gone further in explaining different outcomes, with at least one example perhaps from the last round of primary and caucus elections. **c** However, this student has done enough, especially for AO1, to achieve a good A grade with impressive political vocabulary such as open and closed primaries, front-loading and machine politics and a coherent response (AO3).

C-grade answer

(a) Both primaries and caucuses are methods used to select a party's presidential candidate. They have been widely used since the 1968 McGovern–Fraser Commission's recommendations. Primaries are state-wide elections held in the majority of states. A candidate who wins a state primary will receive a number of delegates from that state who will go to the party's national convention and vote for the candidate **a**. Democrats hold proportional primaries, where the candidates get delegates in proportion to the percentage of the state's popular vote. Republicans in some states hold winner-takes-all primaries where, if the candidate wins the primary, they will then win all the state's delegates **b**. There are two kinds of primary: open and closed.

Some states hold caucuses. These differ in that they tend only to be held in geographically large states that are thinly populated. They also involve a series of state-based meetings (which primaries do not have), leading to a vote on the candidate **a**. Whereas certain primaries can attract a representative turnout, and often a high one, most caucuses attract an unrepresentative and low turnout **c**.

(e) **b** This answer drifts in places, particularly in the attention it gives to the differences between party primaries, which was not part of the question, and a much clearer focus is needed on the differences between primaries and caucuses to achieve a higher AO2 mark. **a** There is clear knowledge of both primaries and caucuses which is worthy of AO1 credit, but lack of a clear focus on the question limits both the AO2 mark and the AO3 communication mark. **c** The last paragraph does bring the answer back to the question with some AO2 analysis and if this paragraph had been developed further, particularly with the use of examples and evidence from recent primaries and caucuses, the mark could have been higher than a C.

(b) 'An outdated eighteenth-century device still used for the election of the twenty-first-century president.' Critically assess the role of the Electoral College. (30 marks)

(e) The question calls for a critical assessment, so your answer should work through several problems that are known to be associated with the role of the Electoral College in presidential selection, using evidence and examples wherever possible from past elections. However, the question also allows you to defend the role of the Electoral College, therefore using arguments from both sides of the debate (AO2). Your answer should clearly demonstrate knowledge and understanding of the way the Electoral College actually works (AO1), in order to provide context, as well as explaining why, despite known problems, it is still used, including the difficulties involved in any reform.

A-grade answer

(b) The 2000 election clearly showed the Electoral College (EC) to be the main factor in the election of the president. Due to the closeness of Bush and Gore in Florida the president was essentially chosen by the voters in that state, and only 500 votes separated the two. When we also remember that Bush, the victor, actually gained fewer popular votes than Gore, we can see that the EC has the potential to distort the public will **b d e**.

The EC is undoubtedly an antiquated device. The Founding Fathers devised it to ensure that the general voting population didn't have too much power. Of course, since then the EC has become much more democratic **a**. All of the electors, with only a rare transgressor, vote for the candidate that their state has voted for **d**.

So the system has been changed to ensure that voters actually have an impact on the decision. Having removed the original purpose of the system — to limit the impact of voters — the USA is now left with a pointless device that distorts public opinion for choosing its chief executive.

The EC system converts the public vote in each state into EC votes. Most states give all their votes to one candidate (although Maine and Nebraska allocate them proportionately), which means that someone who gains 51% of the vote in a state carries 100% of the EC votes of that state, with nothing for the loser **b**.

Although it is clear that there are problems with this system, we must also remember that there are reasons why it remains in place **c**. The central reason goes back to the creation of the system in eighteenth-century Philadelphia. The major conflict when the American Constitution was being drawn up was the extent to which the federal government had power over the individual states **a**. Because of the fear that states would lose their power, a number of concessions were made to the smaller states **c**. First, each state was given equal representation in the Senate, regardless of size or population. To ensure that small states did not then wield disproportionate influence, the House of Representatives was apportioned seats on the basis of population **b**. As the number of EC votes per state is dependent on the number of Congressmen in each state, even the smallest state is assured 3 votes in the EC, with the largest state, California, having 55. The magic number needed to win is 270 out of 538, and this can be achieved by winning as many states as possible, especially the ones with large EC votes **b**. This means that candidates concentrate their campaigning strategies on these crucial states and try to appeal to the voters within them **c**.

The EC system ensures that the smaller states are not totally ignored, yet even this idea can be seen as outdated, as it limits the voting power of those who live in the states with larger populations **c**. A voter in Wyoming actually has more power over who wins their state than a voter in California. However, candidates are obviously going to concentrate more of their efforts on winning bigger states, particularly the swing states **e** such as Ohio as their large number of EC votes — and the fact that they can go either way — gives them a much greater chance of winning the presidency **c**.

Although there are both advantages and disadvantages to a system that allows smaller states to have at least some impact on the outcome, it is hard to argue that people were happy that 2000 saw the most popular candidate in the country defeated and a president elected without a clear popular mandate **d**.

However, we must remember that this is a rarity. The last time it occurred before 2000 was in 1888 **a b**. Since then, the only distortion of the result by the EC had seemed to be in giving the winner a greater margin of victory, so there is little urgency in calls to change the system **c**. It can be said in defence of the EC that in the fragmented political landscape of the USA **e** it provides a basis of stability by helping to eliminate third-party candidates who cannot win concentrated support c and by giving one candidate a clear-cut majority and the legitimacy and mandate to rule c. However, it is hard to imagine how people would feel if the next election saw the leader of the free world chosen by the elected representatives in the House despite the fact that a majority of voters in the country as a whole had clearly chosen one candidate over the other.

Finally, it can be argued that perhaps there is a place for the EC in twenty-first-century US politics, although it may need reforming in the future if problems such as those of 2000 recur.

😊 a This student is able to place the Electoral College in a historical context to explain its workings, demonstrating contextual and historical awareness, and b there is clear understanding of the way that it works to elect the president, so AO1 marks would be high. c There is a good attempt to provide a critical evaluation through analysis of the workings of the EC, although d there are some undeveloped explanations, such as why some rogue electors do not vote the way their state does and why this is criticised, and how and why the EC system distorts the popular will. Generally, though, the response is focused and analytical and attempts to present both sides of the argument, with supporting evidence, thus achieving good AO2 marks. e The use of impressive and relevant political vocabulary, such as popular mandate, campaigning strategies, swing states and fragmented political landscape also raises the AO3 communication mark. Some parts of the answer lack development and clear explanation, but overall the response would certainly be worthy of an A grade.

C-grade answer

(b) The Electoral College (EC) has been widely criticised as a way of electing the president of the USA. It can cause a distortion of results through allowing a candidate with fewer overall votes to win, giving smaller parties little representation, and putting the election in the hands of electors who cast their respective votes.

Each state is assigned a certain amount of EC votes, depending on its population. By itself this is the fairest method of doing things. The number of votes for each presidential candidate is totalled, and the candidate with the most votes is assigned all of the EC votes for that particular state a. This means that a candidate can receive, for example, ten fewer votes out of 1 million than the other candidate and receive no seats whatsoever for that achievement b. The candidate with the highest number of EC votes wins the election. A few weeks after the election, with the results in, electors for each state, who are party members or officials, will meet in the capital of the state. Each will cast their EC vote depending on who won the state. However, electors are not required by law to vote for who actually won the state a. They can vote for whoever they please, so the trust of a large number of voters in a state is put in one person who may turn out to be a 'faithless elector' and vote for an entirely different candidate c.

The first major criticism of the EC system is that an overall winner, with the largest amount of votes in the country, can lose the election to someone who has won more votes in the EC. This happened in the 2000 election between Bush and Gore.

Gore received more votes overall, but Bush performed better in terms of the EC and so won the presidential election. Due to complications in Florida over votes, the decision was taken to the Supreme Court, which ruled in favour of Bush **c**.

This brings me to the problem of getting rid of the EC. The fact is that because the EC was written into the constitution in the eighteenth century, it requires an amendment to change it, which is extremely difficult. An amendment to the constitution also requires that two-thirds of Congress and three-quarters of the states agree to it before it can be implemented. Therefore, it seems as though there is no alternative to the EC at the moment **c**.

Another drawback of the EC is that smaller parties get little or no representation **b**. Their support is scattered across the country, and unlike the Democrats and Republicans, who have strongholds in particular areas, they do not have enough concentrated support in one area to win a state and receive the EC votes. For example, in 2000 Ralph Nader received 19% of the overall votes but received a tiny proportion of representation because of it **d**.

Is the EC outdated now, or has it simply always been as distorting and unfair as this? What alternatives are there?

It could be argued that the world as a whole, and therefore the USA too, is more liberal than it was in the eighteenth century. Therefore, electors in the eighteenth century may not have exercised the 'freedom of speech' now exercised by the 'faithless electors', however rare they are **c**.

Three hundred years do not change the fact that the EC will distort results — the same system is still used. Therefore, it may not be a fair argument to say that the twenty-first century requires a better system than the eighteenth century did — the same problems are still there.

The EC does act like a first-past-the-post system, but only within each state and in a more distorting way than a simple first-past-the-post system. The beauty of a first-past-the-post system is that it is simple for voters to understand: they just cast their vote and hope their candidate wins the state. A straightforward first-past-the-post system like the UK's would not help the situation of the USA too much and would not be worth the effort of implementing it **b**. However, any other system of electing may be harder for voters to understand and may lower turnout further. Therefore, it seems that the USA is stuck with the EC.

In conclusion, I would not necessarily agree that the system is outdated. It has generally presented the same problems today as it would have done 300 years ago — distortion of results, faithless electors and little representation of smaller parties.

However, it is hard to suggest an alternative, as the constitution implements the EC and is very difficult to change. Even if there were an alternative it might not be any better than the current system and would present problems of its own **e**.

ⓔ This student produces a very mixed response to the question: **a** there is accuracy on some of the workings of the Electoral College and a clear attempt to engage with the question, but at the same time there is little coherent structure or developed analysis, however good some of the specific arguments are. **b** At times there is little clarity of argument, such as the mention of presidential candidates winning 'seats' or the arguments relating to first-past-the-post or why the system produces distortions. Also, it is not a problem that minor parties are 'unrepresented', as there is only one president. **c** Other arguments are not fully developed: for example, why are 'faithless electors' criticised, what caused the result in 2000, and why would a constitutional amendment be hard to achieve? **d** There are some factual errors (e.g. Nader's 19% of the vote in 2000), all of which suggest a less than firm grasp of the EC system. **e** The conclusion is very vague. Nevertheless, the student manages to get across just enough AO1 knowledge and AO2 critical assessment to reach a low C grade, although the communication mark (AO3) would not be high.

Question 2 **Political parties**

(a) Why are US parties often described as 'organisationally weak'?   (10 marks)

The answer to this question should focus on the relative weakness of US parties as decentralised organisations (possibly compared with the stronger, centralised UK parties), with some evidence of this weakness, such as their lack of control over candidate selection or over their elected candidates. No reference to party ideology or party renewal is required. An explanation of why parties are weak organisations in the USA, such as the constitutional separation of powers or federalism, would be essential for the higher mark bands.

A-grade answer

(a) The doctrine of the separation of powers and the system of federalism used in the USA encourage political parties that may be considered 'organisationally weak' **b**. In the USA there is a significant fragmentation of power **d** (introduced by the Founding Fathers in order to ensure no area of government dominated the political process), and consequently parties are forced to span a wide range of political institutions **b**. At a state level, parties need representatives, e.g. as governors or in state legislatures, yet equally parties have to make their mark in Washington at the federal level **a**. Parties in the USA must make their voices heard in the federal legislature and gain a hold over the executive, i.e. the presidency. This is not helped by the fact that like the UK, the USA has a bicameral legislature, i.e. the House of Representatives and the Senate. In order to exert most influence, political parties must gain power at all levels of government. As a result the party machine must be incredibly vast, which leads to organisational weaknesses **b**.

The need for a large party machine is enhanced by America's geography. The USA is a huge area, which means parties have to work hard to cover the whole country. In covering all areas geographically and politically, the party inevitably becomes fragmented **b**. Moreover, it is noteworthy that major parties meet in their entirety only once every 4 years, at the national party convention during a presidential election. This event has been declining in significance in recent years and consequently there is little opportunity for party unity to be significantly strengthened; the focus, after all, is on the selection of a president, not the day-to-day running of the party **a**.

Finally, weak party discipline in the USA would encourage the idea of ineffective party organisation **a**. Voting across party lines in Congress is common (although reduced in recent years), demonstrating that US parties are relatively uncoordinated. This is unlike the UK, where strict party discipline is enforced via the party whips **c**.

Although there are reasons for organisationally weak parties in the USA, there is also an argument that this is necessary. US parties are essentially 'broad coalitions': they contain, for example, moderates like McCain (Republican) and Obama (Democrat), while also having a more conservative wing. Essentially, therefore, stronger party organisation would give parties a narrower appeal and as a consequence potentially alienate large 'voting blocs' or proportions of the electorate **b d**.

It has therefore been argued that symptoms of weak organisation, e.g. issue-centred or candidate-centred election campaigns **a d** are deliberate, as parties attempt to gain a maximum number of votes.

Historically, the American parties have always encompassed a range of diverse groups spanning the entire country, e.g. the New Deal policies of Roosevelt in the 1930s, uniting white southerners, African-Americans and blue-collar manual workers. Consequently, it can be argued parties may appear organisationally weak yet it would be impossible to perceive any other alternative, considering the nature of the Constitution (separation of powers) and the previous success of parties acting as 'broad coalitions' or 'big umbrellas' **d**.

e This student's answer is a strongly analytical response covering a lot of ground. **b** It clearly shows why parties are weaker in the USA, thus gaining AO2 marks, and **a** demonstrates AO1 knowledge of some (but not all) of their organisational characteristics. The student backs up the arguments with convincing evidence and wide-ranging examples, and **c** also makes a synoptic passing reference to the UK for comparison. **d** The answer is communicated coherently and with structure, including excellent political vocabulary such as fragmentation of power, issue and candidate-centred campaigns and broad coalitions, although it could have been more succinct in parts. It would achieve a high grade A.

C-grade answer

(a) The best expression of national organisation by the two US parties comes in the national conventions, the most public manifestation of the parties. Although the conventions show organisation, they only occur every 4 years, lasting for 4 days, and there is not much opportunity for all the 4,000 delegates who attend to have their say **a**. Despite being organised to pick the presidential candidate and the running mate and to decide the party platform, the convention has become less formal and less important. The decline in organisation may be a result of their diminishing importance: it is suggested they merely confirm the presidential candidate and running mate. Their poor organisation can be seen in the fact that in 1963 the terrestrial channels put in 46 hours of coverage of the Republican convention, while in 2000 the same channels managed just 10.5 hours!

The national conventions are also used to decide the party platform, but the weak organisation of this was shown in 1992. One of the planks of the Republican Party platform was 'We believe the unborn child has a fundamental right to life,' but they then went on to call for a human life amendment to the Constitution. A CBS poll found that only 7% of voters approved of this plank, thus the convention was organised well enough to be able to make unpopular decisions to go on the party platform **a**.

Parties' main functions are fund-raising, organisation, communication and policy formation **a** but their failure to fulfil these functions means they have to some extent been usurped by pressure groups, political action committees and the media. The weak organisation of the parties has to some extent been forgotten about, in that politicians communicate to the voters through the media and the voters speak back to them through opinion polls, so the role of the parties is cut out **a**.

ⓔ **a** Despite initially focusing the answer almost exclusively on the roles of the national conventions, meaning a very limited response, the student does demonstrate some AO1 knowledge of party organisation through this description. However, the answer does not really get to grips with the wider question, showing little AO2 analysis of why parties are organisationally weaker in the USA and not giving evidence to show that they are by indicating other organisational characteristics. Although the last paragraph makes enough valid and creditable points, and demonstrates sufficient knowledge of party conventions, to just reach a low grade C, overall the answer lacks the clear and convincing understanding of the main reasons for party weakness which could have gained higher AO2 marks and led to a higher grade. The answer could also have been more clearly communicated to achieve higher AO3 communication marks.

**(b) Consider the reasons for the strength of the two-party system
and the insignificance of third parties in the USA.** (30 marks)

ⓔ In your response you should give reasons why, in a country as large and diverse as the USA, there are only two parties effectively competing at all levels of government. Answers should span a number of different explanations, from the strength of partisan identification through to funding advantages, the 'big tent' nature of the parties and the effects of the electoral system. Examples and evidence are expected in support of both two-party strength and third-party insignificance in elections. However, students at the higher levels of response may challenge either the insignificance of third parties, by pointing to their successes or impact, or the strength of the two-party system, by noting that (unlike the position in the UK) the two main parties are very different in each of the 50 states.

A-grade answer

(b) Although it is certainly true that a key characteristic of the US political system has been the insignificance of third-party candidates, it is possible to argue that in some cases they do succeed in their aims, and that the two-party political system is not as strong as it might seem **b**.

First, let us consider the evidence in favour of the strength of the two-party system. It should be noted that not since 1856 has a president not been a member of either the Democratic or Republican party **a**. Furthermore, these two parties currently dominate the federal legislature. Out of 100 senators, only one remains independent, having defected from the Democratic Party, and only one of 435 members of the House is independent of the two main parties **a**. This clearly indicates that the two major parties have maintained their strength, but the question this raises is: why?

Perhaps the most obvious reason is the first-past-the-post electoral system used in all US elections. According to this system, all seats (and Electoral College votes) are awarded to the candidate who gets the most votes. This means that third parties are at a tremendous disadvantage, for even if they gain a substantial portion of the vote they are unlikely to achieve any seats in the legislature or votes for the presidency **b**. For example, although Ross Perot gained 19% of the vote in the presidential election of 1992, he was not able to win any Electoral College votes at all **a**. The only small parties that do gain from this system are the regionally based parties, as they can rely on concentrated support **a b**. Thus in

1968, George Wallace and the American Independence Party gained 13% of the vote and 45 Electoral College votes, as they were able to hold much of the South a. Because of the regional nature of these parties, they cannot hope to gain enough broad support to challenge either the Republicans or the Democrats, and so the first-past-the-post system has been of tremendous benefit to the strength of the two-party system b c.

Another significant factor in this success has been the flexibility of the two main parties working over huge geographical areas, with one of the most diverse populations on earth a. The USA's Democratic and Republican parties cover a whole range of interests and political philosophies. Both parties have liberal and conservative wings, and so can appeal to broad sections of the public b c. Third parties such as the Socialists or the Constitution Party tend to be on the fringes of the US political scene and find it difficult to convince enough of the electorate to support them a.

Furthermore, the political system itself favours the Democrats and Republicans and the preservation of the two-party system in a number of ways.

First, states have many different rules regarding who gets to appear on the ballot. While it is possible to appear on the ballot in Alabama with 25 signatures, other states require a much higher figure or even a percentage (e.g. 5%) of the state's population a. For an unknown party this can be very difficult, as it means collecting millions of signatures and spending huge amounts of money, usually with little to show for it b.

This leads to the issue of campaign finance. It is not possible to gain matched funding c from the federal government unless you have gained 5% of the popular vote at the last election a. This means that while the two big parties always gain funding, a party would have to have been successful in a previous election before it could gain enough votes or money to be successful b. In other words, the system is heavily disadvantageous for third parties and clearly favours the two main parties. Only Ross Perot and the Reform Party have been able to claim funding, and then only in 1996 and 2000 a.

Beyond this there are other factors at work, and it is very difficult for a third party to gain enough money from private donors to establish itself. As the system and structure of American politics and society is so disadvantageous b few are likely to give resources or financial assistance: it would mean backing an almost certain loser. But until they gain such financial assistance, third parties are likely to continue to lose b.

The media too have not been helpful to third parties and have tended to reinforce the strength of the two-party system. The media, particularly the television networks and cable channels such as NBC and CNN, are unlikely to mention candidates from smaller parties, as they cannot see them as successful a. Such candidates consequently find it much more difficult to get their message across than the Republicans and the Democrats b. Furthermore, only once has a presidential candidate from outside the two main parties been able to take part in a presidential debate, and since then the American people have only been presented with a simple choice between two candidates a. Additionally, the cost of television advertising (unlike the UK, the US system offers no free broadcasting time for parties) makes it difficult for parties already starved of funds to gain public attention b.

One reason why all these disadvantages have remained in place is the difficulty in bringing about change in the USA. In order to remove many of these obstacles to third parties, for example introducing a presidential election system without the distorting EC, would require either a constitutional amendment or successful votes in the states, both notoriously difficult to achieve a b. Even after talks about change following the Gore–Bush controversy in 2000, little has been done to make serious reforms, as the current system benefits the two main parties so much b.

Finally, many in America consider the two-party system desirable as it ensures (usually) a winner who gets more than 50% of the vote. Since 1916 the Republicans and the Democrats have never had less than 80% of the vote between them, which is in stark contrast to the 60–65% attained by Labour and the Conservatives in the UK d. In such a large and diverse country, many consider it preferable to have an obvious winner with a majority, as it promotes consensus c and this can only be attained in a two-party system.

In conclusion, although some argue America is not a two-party system, but is instead perhaps a 100-party system, it is undeniable that the strength and durability of the Republican and Democratic dominance of US politics has survived because of the system, media, money and ideology e.

e b This is a very well-focused and wide-ranging response to the question, and the focus, which starts in the introduction, is maintained throughout the essay, which has a coherent structure (AO3) and contains a lot of convincing AO2 analysis and evaluation. a The AO1 knowledge and understanding is impressive and d the response includes synoptic reference to the UK for comparison, with almost every argument backed up by relevant evidence and examples of both the two main parties and a number of different third parties and their impact. The answer is very well communicated, c using political concepts and vocabulary, and e culminates in a conclusion, so the AO3 mark would be high. This answer would gain a high grade A.

C-grade answer

(b) The USA has always had a two-party system. From the historic days of Washington and Jefferson establishing the two parties, third parties or Independents have never had any influence, and although recent years have seen attempts to achieve this, e.g. by Ross Perot (19%), the restriction of the electoral system and broad coalitions have stopped this. In the light of this, can the US system be deemed a two-party system, or are third parties slowly gaining more popularity?

In the two parties of Democrats and Republicans numerous factions appear. As Bennett said, you don't just get 'Democrats' or 'Republicans' as party labels. Many are termed 'liberal Democrats' or 'conservative Republicans', and in 2000 Bush called himself a 'compassionate conservative' a. This demonstrates the 'broad church' system of the two parties which enables them to exclude third parties that cannot fit their policies into an ideological gap in the US electorate b. From the Rockefeller Republicans to the conservative Republicans to the southern Democrats (Clinton and Gore) to the old left (Dukakis), all the parties have internal conflicting factions representing different ideologies a. Rockefellers such as Ford were more Democrat-inclined, promoting bigger government etc. However, you also had the conservatives like Reagan etc. who were more traditional Republicans, believing in tax cuts etc. A recent development of the Democrats with Clinton's New Deal d demonstrated the centralisation of the two main parties, with Clinton trying to get rid of 'big government' under the influence of growing public opinion, giving substance to Mark Shields' point that 'they are two parties separated by the issue of abortion'.

It is this ideological engulfment of the whole US electoral spectrum that prevents third-party success but also ensures their durability b. When Anderson was campaigning in 1980, President Nixon announced the 'southern strategy' to attract all his voters d. The same thing happened with Ross Perot, which made Clinton and others do lots of reforms, so that his popularity suffered heavily.

However, is this insignificance of third parties really true? In recent years, since the time of Anderson, third-party candidates have in turn affected and influenced the vote. In 1992 Perot took a lot of Republican voters, resulting in a Democrat victory, while Nader in 2004, while only gaining 1%, still managed to take vital votes in a tight race of 271–266 a d!

It can be said that third parties never intend to be that significant and most are just temporary, created to provide an outlet for disillusioned voters (with the exception of Ross Perot in 1992 and 1996) b.

However, is this attitude of just influencing and being more like electoral pressure groups b than political parties forced by the restrictions of the US system? It can be said that the Electoral College system actually is not in proportion to the amount of votes won. Ross Perot gained 19% of the vote but because they were evenly spread over states he gained no Electoral College votes a. One governor did manage to gain 13 EC votes, mainly because his vote was concentrated in the southern states, which still didn't make a significant impact. Reforms such as the Maine system and automatic plan didn't even give much hope for any renewed third-party significance.

However, can we ever deem the American system a two-party system, with Broder actually stating 'the party's over'? This expands on the fact that the USA can be seen as a 50-party system. Federalism and state powers and the fact that they only meet nationally every 4 years means that they can be split up into geographical factions, as the Republicans' policy in Arkansas will be different to that in Connecticut a b. One case study showed that they declared in Arkansas 'protection for all God-fearing families', but Connecticut watered down these policies and promised 'good education'!

But is this such a big problem in America? The liberal democracy and the Constitution ensure that Congressmen are elected on issue lines more than on party lines, unlike MPs in the UK. This brings in Edmund Burke's theory of representative or delegate. As one political scientist said, Congressmen 'take party lines first, but they become second when the election is over' and constituent pressure is much more of an issue c.

Though there are some claims of party renewal, many claim that the DRC for Democrats and Bill Frist's national campaigning in 2002 have helped to develop the parties c.

The American Congress shows the US system is not that of party government, and carrots and sticks cannot be used to such a high degree as in the UK, so despite their presence the American system can be said to force this culture of 'broad church' parties and that of insignificant third parties. What can be said of both political cultures is that despite their differences the significance of third parties is rising, with the UK's Liberal Democrats gaining their highest number of seats in 2005 (66) and Ross Perot and Nader in the USA causing some interesting results e. This may indicate the changing scene of both party systems and their prospective durability.

ⓔ Although this answer would not gain high AO3 marks for communication, as it is not well structured or fully coherent, it does attempt to communicate some interesting and relevant AO2 arguments. However, most of these remain undeveloped. The student has a lot of knowledge but **c** it is not always directly linked to the question and frequently drifts (e.g. into Burke's theory or Electoral College reform) and arguments only tenuously related to the question are introduced, such as party decline and renewal. **d** It also contains several errors, such as 'Clinton's New Deal', Nixon's southern strategy in 1980, and Nader's 2004 result. However, there is relevant analysis in the answer, such as **b** the broad church nature of the parties and the electoral system effect, backed up with relevant examples (Perot and Nader) and **a** using specific evidence from voting statistics, as well as **e** an attempt to bring in some comparative material from the UK. This just pushes this answer into the C grade. Higher marks could have been achieved if the student had focused more on the actual question and excluded scattergun arguments lacking relevance to the question, which apart from wasting precious time indicate a lack of understanding of what the question is asking the student to do. Some parts of the answer would have been more relevant to (a) than (b), but they cannot be allocated marks if they are in the wrong section.

Question 3 Voting behaviour

(a) How important is party identification (partisanship) in explaining US voting behaviour?

(10 marks)

(e) This question calls for a clear definition and explanation of the term itself and a focus on why and whether it is important in explaining why Americans vote the way they do. It demands some knowledge of the long-term (primacy) factors affecting voting behaviour and the agencies of political socialisation, and also some evidence of the decline of partisanship in recent years, with some explanation offered for this decline and its possible consequences in order to address the 'how important' part of the question.

A-grade answer

(a) The majority of American voters have some form of long-term party identification, which is described as a deep-rooted attachment to one political party **a**. It is usually connected to a voter's political socialisation within the family leading them to become a Democrat or a Republican and subsequently to vote for that party throughout their life **a**. Party identification can be very strong, with the voter having a party loyalty throughout their life, or it can weaken as a result of other influences on their political thinking and behaviour, for example from their education or their occupation or from the influence of specific candidates or issues at elections, which may result in them changing their vote **a b**.

For example, it was said that many Democrats switched their vote to Reagan in 1980 and 1984 because they liked his personality and his right-wing policies more than they did the Democrat ones. They were known as 'Reagan Democrats' **a c**. This weakening of party identification is called de-alignment **c**. Voters without a party identification are called Independents **c** — their vote can go either way, and both parties try to attract support from these voters while at the same time trying to keep the votes of their 'core' aligned supporters **a c**. It is thought that the number of independent voters fluctuates from election to election.

An example of voters with a strong party identification would have been southern Democrat voters until the 1960s, when they lost their strong identification with the Democratic Party because of its commitment to Civil Rights **a b**. Since that time, many white southern voters have identified with and switched to voting for the Republican Party. Because many voters now lack a strong identification with a party, they are less likely to turn out to vote, which has led to higher abstention in recent years **b**. This is particularly true of 'weak' identifiers rather than 'strong' ones. Because US political parties are aware that partisanship is weakening in the electorate, they cannot rely on a solid base of voters turning out to vote for them. Their candidates now have to work harder to keep the support not only of their own voters but also of the de-aligned independent voters at each election **b c**.

(e) This is an exceptionally well-argued response, demonstrating **a** a very clear understanding of the term, and is well communicated, with **c** use of political terms and concepts. It does not drift from the question, **b** addresses AO2 'importance' and remains focused throughout. Although no statistical evidence is presented, this does not detract from the answer overall, which contains strong evidence and examples of partisanship as well as its decline. It would receive a very high mark for all three assessment objectives and a top A grade.

C-grade answer

(a) Party identification is when voters link to parties and always vote for those parties no matter who the candidates are or what the issues are at that election **a**. Voters get their party identification from different things like their class or where they live in the USA, in the red states or the blue states **a**. Voters who are poor and have little education are likely to identify with the Democratic Party, as this is the one most likely to help them. Voters who come from richer classes and who have gone to university are more likely to be Republicans as they support lower taxes **a**.

American voters do not always keep a strong identification with a party, their circumstances may change and they may change their vote as a result. Women are more likely to be Democrat voters, but sometimes they switch to the Republicans because they do not agree with abortion or they are concerned about national security, like the 'security moms' who voted for Bush in 2004 **a**. However, most voters do identify with one party rather than another and will usually vote for that party, and if they are very strongly identified with a particular party they are never likely to change their voting behaviour. If parties do not manage to get their identified voters to turn out to vote it is possible that they will lose the election. That is why they concentrate on pleasing their voters rather than trying to win votes from the 'other side' in their campaigns **b**.

(e) **a** While this answer does not fully explain the sources of partisan alignment and identification, it does try to explain the term and gives examples of aligned voters. **b** It is also quite focused, but it lacks the extra analysis and evidence, political vocabulary and communication that would take it into higher assessment objective levels. It would, however, gain a C grade largely as a result of the AO1 marks.

(b) Explain the causes and consequences of split-ticket voting in US elections.

(30 marks)

(e) This is, in effect, a two-part question with focus both on the causes and consequences of the phenomenon of split-ticket voting in the USA, and although it is not necessary to deal with both aspects equally, both must be addressed to access the higher mark bands. The extent of split-ticket voting is different at each election, and you should provide evidence of it occurring and explain why its incidence changes from election to election, to illustrate understanding. A top response would give several reasons why voters split their tickets, and several consequences of this, along with a clear definition of the term.

A-grade answer

(b) Split-ticket voting (STV) may seem to an observer to be the illogical act of a confused or unintelligent electorate, but in truth it is more due to voter sophistication and rational choice **a** plus a variety of other reasons. There are many consequences of STV and they are arguably good or bad, depending on viewpoint.

Split-ticket voting is the act of voting for candidates of different parties at different levels of government in the same election cycle **a**. The main cause is partisan de-alignment with voters identifying less and less with one particular party **b c**. The study *The American Voter*, published in 1960, identified three types of elections: realigning elections, reinforcing elections and anomalous elections **a**. Since this study, thanks mainly to the strange results of elections in the 1970s and the rise of STV, many commentators have come to believe that the USA is in a period of de-alignment rather than realignment **c**. Party identification statistics from the 1950s showed over 90% identification with one of the two main parties, but voter identification statistics more recently show over 20% of voters describe themselves as Independents **a**. The net result of this is that these voters will happily vote for one party for one office and another party for another, at the same time, regardless of ideology **b**.

The American Voter model also saw the citizens as unsophisticated viewers of politics, unable to grasp political ideas. This has definitely changed, with voters now clearly able to distinguish between the parties. This would indicate the 'rational choice' theory for explaining STV, according to which voters are sophisticated enough to choose deliberately between different candidates for different offices **b c**. There are many reasons why they might do this: for example they might look for different qualities for different posts, voting for a Republican president strong on foreign policy and a Democratic Congressman better able to bring benefits to the state or district **b**.

There are two other factors that can explain STV that are strongly linked: the incumbency factor and pork-barrelling. The incumbency factor refers to the fact that US politicians already in post are rarely defeated when they face re-election. This is linked to pork-barrelling, the term that describes a member of Congress attempting to secure money, jobs or other benefits for their state **b c**. These two combined factors mean that voters are more likely to split their ticket and vote for a member of another party because he or she is a reputable incumbent who has provided generously for the constituency, while voting for a different party's candidate for the presidency.

The effects of STV are important and threefold **b**. The first is divided government **b c**. In the first 70 years of the twentieth century there were only 4 years when different parties controlled the Congress and the White House. In the last 30 years of the twentieth century there were only 4 years when there was not divided government **a**. After the 2004 election there was united government, with the Republican Party controlling both the executive and the legislature. Divided government is the obvious result of STV if enough voters vote against their own party at different levels of government.

The other two effects of STV are also by-products of divided government **b**. Gridlock is the term used to describe a period when laws are difficult to pass because of party differences between the executive and the legislature or even between the two houses of the legislature **c**. Obviously, if the two houses are controlled by different parties, gridlock is much more likely **b**. However, this is not always the case: even with united government in 1992–94 Clinton suffered gridlock with his healthcare reforms.

The other effect of STV is the system of checks and balances between the three branches of government. If the two elected branches are controlled by different parties, they will check and balance one another much more effectively. Voters may be voting for these checks to take place **b**.

STV emerged from a period of political disillusionment in the 1970s **a** and its results have been widespread and noticeable. Accompanying the growing sophistication of the American voter has been the rise of candidate and issue voting, whereby voters will vote for a presidential candidate because of their personal qualities or because they support a particular issue, e.g. abortion, while continuing to support the other party for Congress **b**. This is exemplified by John McCain, who gained over 70% of the vote in Arizona, a state only slightly Republican in its voting for other offices. He may have won these votes because he was a Republican who supported campaign finance reform and was pro-choice **a b**. The importance of rising issue voting was seen in the 1980s, when many Democrats, called 'Reagan Democrats', voted for Reagan because of his personality but also because of his popular aversion to 'big government' at the time **c**.

ⓔ Although lacking a reasoned conclusion, this is a very well-focused and coherent response, giving **b** a theoretical perspective on voting behaviour, **a** a clear understanding of the term and reference to psephological models and theories such as rational choice and the American voter model. It does not drift from the question and **b** the analytical and evaluative explanations remain clear throughout, raising the AO2 mark, while **c** excellent use of political language such as de-alignment, gridlock, divided government, incumbency and pork-barrelling raises the AO3 mark. **c** The evidence and examples used, such as the Reagan Democrats, are convincing and consistent, leading to a solid A grade. Some attempt at explaining why American voters can split their ticket, such as the federal system or the separation of powers, would have shown contextual awareness, while the introduction of specific statistical evidence of split-ticket voting would have pushed the mark to the top of Level 4.

C-grade answer

(b) Split-ticket voting has increased enormously on a national and state level, which has far-reaching consequences as it has resulted in the theory of party decline **a**. In contrast to UK elections, US campaigns tend to be far more candidate-centred and party label counts for less **c**. Nationally, President Bill Clinton (1992–2000) was the victim of split-ticket voting and it hindered his ability to have legislation passed. In 1999–2000 he was the president but faced a Republican Congress with a majority in both the House and the Senate. Consequently it was far more difficult for him to have legislation passed, as Republicans are far more conservative than even the conservative Democrats. The Congress was likely to veto countless acts **a**.

The mid-term elections also affect split-ticket voting. For instance, in 2002, Kansas elected a Republican Senator, Pat Roberts, but a Democrat as Governor, Kathleen Sibelius. So even at a state level, there are likely to be conflicts **a**.

Another reason why so many US voters split their ticket when voting is that certain candidates have the advantage of incumbency and length of terms. Once a Senator has been elected she/he has 6 years to build up their reputation. Americans like to back winners, and so despite party identification it is more likely that they will vote for the incumbent **b**. This was reflected in the 1994 mid-term elections, in which no Republican incumbents who sought re-election lost in a single House or Senate race. Strom Thurmond, for example, was originally elected in 1954 and only retired at the age of 100! **d**.

Parties are very weak in American politics and so the party label does not stand for much. As partisan alignment has fallen dramatically over the years **c** and split-ticket voting has more than doubled since the 1950s, this emphasises the fact that a number of other reasons has resulted in split-ticket voting going up. Short-term factors are now incredibly important, such as the current state of the economy **c**. In 1980 Reagan defeated President Carter by getting the voters to focus on just one question, 'Are you better off than you were 4 years ago?' **d**.

Image is also important, and therefore the media also play an important part. Events leading up to the election are critical **c** while the prime minister in the UK has the luxury of setting the election date within a 5-year term, the president does not enjoy this benefit. For instance, had the 1992 presidential election taken place just one year earlier, George H. W. Bush would have defeated Bill Clinton, as he was riding on high approval as a result of the Gulf War **d**.

National party conventions can also be important. In 1992, Bush was challenged by Buchanan. This was televised and showed the internal factions within the Republican Party. Voters who watched this may have decided to switch their vote. Therefore internal factions can influence voting **d**.

Another reason is that voters may not see a big difference between the two major parties. As Lord Bryce stated, 'They are like liquor bottles, each denoting the kind of liquor they contain, but both are empty **d**.'

This illustrates the view of many people who feel that the two main parties are very similar to one another, except in image **d**.

The consequences of split-ticket voting nationally were quite large, as it is very hard for the executive to dominate when the legislature is predominantly of the opposing party. Therefore it is extremely difficult to have legislation passed, unlike in the UK **b**. (Unfinished)

e **a** The lack of a clear definition of what split-ticket voting actually is and the vagueness of the first paragraph leads to confusion in the answer, and while many valid points are made about voting behaviour generally, they do not fully connect to the question asked, thus failing to gain credit. **b** The argument on the incumbency factor is not fully developed to show that some members of Congress can keep their seats even when there is a landslide vote for the opposing party for president, as happened for example in 1984 and 1996, because of the incumbency factor or successful pork-barrelling for 'the folks back home'. **c** The links made with candidate-centred campaigns, the decline in partisan identification, the growing importance of short-term factors and the importance of the media influencing voters gain AO2 marks, but the student could have raised the mark by developing them further, making them clearer and providing some supporting examples. **d** At times this answer is over-generalised, simply looking at factors influencing voting or focusing on the parties themselves rather than explaining split-ticket voting and its consequences.

Some limited knowledge of the causes of split-ticket voting and some attempt at explanation of its effects **b** allow this answer just to reach a C grade, but it achieves a higher mark for knowledge (AO1) than for analysis (AO2), and the AO3 mark is low because clarity and focus is lacking in the answer.

Question 4 **Pressure groups**

(a) Explain the growth of pressure group activity in recent years.   (10 marks)

ⓔ The focus here must be on reasons for the increased activity of pressure groups in the USA and nothing else. Students may go back to the 1960s, when pressure group activity began to grow significantly, to offer valid explanations for this growth. Examples and evidence of new pressure group activity, such as the civil rights movement, the pro- and anti-abortion groups after *Roe* v *Wade* and new social movements arising from the emergence of political issues such as environmentalism and feminism, should be included in the explanation wherever possible. Any other consideration of pressure group activity is not required and would not be rewarded.

A-grade answer

(a) The growth in pressure group activity, particularly since the 1960s, is the result of many factors. It can certainly be seen as part of a growth of direct democracy with increasing use of initiatives, referendums and notably issue groups **b**. In a climate of falling turnout due to voter apathy and lack of political efficacy, **c** pressure groups seemed set to increase in activity and popularity as they offered an opportunity for genuine participation **b** and the ability to get new issues onto the agenda **b**. For example, Civil Rights legal changes in the 1960s were the work of the National Association for the Advancement of Colored People (NAACP) **a**. This effectiveness of pressure groups increased their popularity and more began to grow **b**. Pressure groups benefited from the numerous access points due to the decentralised federal system and the weak, fragmented party system **d**.

Pressure groups also grew and benefited from the USA's participatory political culture **b c**. Pressure groups benefited at a time when many people were less committed to conventional political activism and participation, as evidenced by partisan de-alignment **b c** (the number of people classifying themselves as Independents rose from 6% to 28% between 1952 and 1992) and by falling turnout and party membership **b**.

The general period of relative affluence and prosperity created by the welfare state allowed and encouraged an emphasis on new environmental and social problems, **b** e.g. the creation of the Sierra Club **a**. This growing concern over new problems replaced the economic worries which had dominated in previous times **b**. Also the growth of 'sleaze' and the decline in the attractiveness of politicians as a result of Nixon and the Watergate scandal in the 1970s led to the trend towards pressure group involvement and other such concerns **e**.

ⓔ **b** Although by no means providing a perfectly focused answer, this student does specifically address the question and is able to offer several different and plausible explanations for the growth of pressure group activity. **a** There is also a good integration of evidence and examples such as the effectiveness of the NAACP and new problems such as environmentalism into the answer, which raises the AO1 and AO2 marks, along with **c** the use of political concepts and political vocabulary. Good analytical points do not need to be over-argued: the argument that the effectiveness of pressure groups increased their popularity is concise and clear, although some other arguments would have benefited from greater clarity and further development, such as **d** the relationship of access points to growth. **e** The linkage of the Watergate scandal to the growth of pressure groups is an interesting one, as is the implied link between falling turnouts and pressure group activity, but both could have been developed further for higher AO2 marks. The range of explanations allows this response to reach a grade A.

C-grade answer

(a) The US federal system creates numerous access points for pressure groups where they can influence politicians, whether it be state legislatures, governors, Congress, the executive or the judiciary **c**. The USA has also always been a country of diverse interests: Floridians have different views to Alaskans, and Californian fruit-pickers have different opinions to Fortune 500 CEOs **c**. Interest groups are one of the only ways that everyone's views can be represented at the same level. Accompanying this is the fact that the two main parties are so broad and catch-all in their nature that they cannot represent the views of all their supporters at one time **b**. The work *The American Voter*, published in 1960, portrayed the US electorate as unsophisticated and generally uninterested in politics. This would change from the 1960s onwards as voters became more sophisticated and were able to clearly distinguish between the parties. This sophistication also led to an increase in the activity of pressure groups as more and more citizens participated through them **b**.

Pressure groups have also benefited from the proliferation of controversial and contentious issues **b** which separate rather than unite parties. Pressure groups campaign over questions such as abortion, gun control, gay rights, Civil Rights, women's rights and the environment. These issues have fuelled the increase in pressure group activity, including such examples as Emily's List, the Sierra Club, the League of Women Voters and many others **a b**.

The increase in PAC activity during the 1970s and 1980s was influenced by the Federal Election Act of 1974 and amendments made to it which eventually created the term 'soft money', whereby they could spend money unregulated by campaign finance laws **c**.

On the whole it is clear that pressure groups have exploded in number and that there has been a variety of causes of this.

e **b** It is clear from the answer that this student has a lot of knowledge of US pressure groups and at times is able to focus this on the question asked, so gaining some AO2 marks. **c** The main problem is the very over-generalised response that relates more to pressure group activity and fails to sustain a clear focus on growth. However, **b** the selection of one or two reasons, such as the growing sophistication of voters and new issues that attracted growing participation in pressure group activity, and **a** the many examples given, take the response into a C grade.

(b) Assess the factors that make some US pressure groups more successful than others in achieving their goals.

(30 marks)

e This question asks students to make evaluative judgements about the variables that influence pressure groups' success (or failure) and to assess the numerous factors involved in explaining why some pressure groups may successfully achieve their goals and others may not, perhaps at different times. It is therefore essential to focus on several factors to explain how and why successful pressure groups do achieve their goals, comparing them with those that are less successful. Examples of specific pressure groups and evidence of their 'successful' or 'unsuccessful' activities within the US political system are essential to achieve higher grades.

A-grade answer

(b) Some US pressure groups have been seen to achieve considerably more success than others. The reasons for such differences can be explained by a number of different factors **b**.

Commonly, the finances of pressure groups, or more specifically their financial wing, political action committees (PACs), and their ability to raise funds are of considerable importance **a**. As the costs of fighting elections increase for both presidential and congressional candidates, the importance of pressure group donations heightens **b**. Concerns over the amount of money contributed to political candidates by PACs were highlighted in the passing of the Federal Election Campaign Act 1974, which placed a number of restrictions on so-called 'hard money' **c**. Notably, any one PAC was prevented from donating more than $5,000 per annum under this legislation. Arguably, though, pressure groups are still able to exert massive influence through 'soft money', used to encourage potential voters for their favoured party to register, for example **a**.

A lot of commentary has highlighted the massive role pressure groups have played in party finance in the past. It has been questioned whether a system of 'cash for access' exists, where greater finances give groups greater political clout **b**. It is true that groups that tend to be more affluent, e.g. large oil companies, do appear to achieve more success. During his presidency George W. Bush was dogged by claims that he was linked too closely with energy corporations and the oil industry. The collapse of Enron is particularly noteworthy, as it highlighted the work Bush had done in commending Enron to the Indian government **d**.

That said, this argument has its critics. In the past, *Fortune* magazine, which conducts an annual survey of the most influential pressure groups, has frequently found that it is membership numbers rather than finance that give some groups the greater advantage **b**. Significantly, the American Association of Retired Persons has 33 million members and is often ranked highest in *Fortune's* survey. This argument is further supported by the relative success of the National Rifle Association, which has a 3 million membership of extremely pro-gun Americans **e**. This group even helped Clinton's legislation introducing a 'cooling off' period for those wishing to purchase guns after the Columbine shootings.

The government in power is a further factor affecting the success of pressure groups. The Republicans, for example, tend to be pro-gun and anti-abortion. A Republican-dominated Congress, therefore, is more likely to listen to the professional lobbying of the NRA or National Right to Life Committee when passing legislation. Notably, pressure group influence on the federal executive is subject to change, depending on the ideological persuasion of the incumbent president **a b**.

Furthermore, if a group can become part of an 'iron triangle' it is likely to exert greater influence. This is the relationship between a pressure group, a congressional committee and a government department, whereby all three work together for mutual benefit. The agricultural industry in particular has been successful in using iron triangles to achieve greater subsidies for farmers, for example **f**.

The cause which a group advocates, such as pro- or anti-environmental concerns, or the kind (rich or poor) or number (many or few) of members that it represents can also have a great influence on its success, e.g. the NAACP, representing black Americans, helped bring about the *Brown* v *Board of Topeka* Supreme Court case in 1954, boosting the success of the Civil Rights Movement **a**.
(Run out of time. Please see bullet points.)

- Media attention to the group, especially if popular, can boost the success of the campaign. Illegal activity can worsen it, e.g. attacks on abortion clinics by pro-life groups in the 1990s **a b**.
- Good leadership, e.g. Charlton Heston, former leader of NRA **a**.
- Good organisation, e.g. organising successful campaigns such as the Million Mom March against guns **a b**.
- Timing and circumstances, e.g. a poor economy making governments less likely to listen to environmental groups such as the Sierra Club wishing to curb industry **a b**.
- A group's use of modern technology, e.g. Christian Coalition successfully used e-mails and phones to rally support to lobby politicians **a b**.
- Conclusion **g** — success depends on a range of factors, circumstances, party in power, strength of membership, whether seen by public as a good cause, all of which are subject to change, therefore changing fortunes of different pressure groups at different times.

ℯ **a** This is a very well-argued, analytical response to the question, with some very impressive AO1 evidence communicated of both success and the lack of it. **b** A clear focus is maintained throughout, apart from **c** a slight drift into campaign finance at the beginning, wasting time which could have been used to finish the essay in continuous prose. The essay shows a clear understanding and AO2 analysis of pressure group politics and variable success, with impressive examples well communicated and integrated into the response. **d** References to Enron and 'cash for access' are particularly impressive as is **e** knowledge of pressure group numbers of the AARP and the NRA. Political concepts are used, such as **f** iron triangles, and AO2 links are made to party ideology and pressure group success. The result is an A-grade response, despite the final important and focused arguments and **g** conclusion being bullet-pointed, which would lower the potential communication (AO3) mark.

C-grade answer

(b) There are certain factors with the USA that make some pressure groups more successful than others. First, one of the most obvious is the actual issue in question. A pressure group that promotes a sympathetic issue is more likely to attain success, as it will gain more public and media attention **a**. For example, the National Right to Life pressure group campaigns on the issue of abortion, a subject that is hotly debated in the USA, which allows them to attain more success **a**.

Furthermore, finance is an issue that has a massive role within the US pressure group system. Pressure groups use political action committees to elect and defeat candidates, fund attack adverts and so on. These PACs are highly professional and highly organised in the political marketplace. They bid for power and success within US politics, and ultimately the pressure groups that can 'buy' the best Congressmen enjoy the most success. For example, Bush was coined the 'Toxic Texan' due to his links with the oil industry **b**.

However, the Christian Coalition and the American Association of Retired Persons do not use PACs, as finance is not considered a major player in pressure group politics. Both the Christian Coalition and the AARP have mass membership, which is seen as more influential than money. The AARP has a membership of 33 million, which is used to threaten politicians (note that voting turnout among 'grey voters' is extremely high). Politicians cannot afford to lose such massive chunks of voters, especially as US elections are becoming closer and closer (*Bush v Gore* in 2000, for instance), and therefore these pressure groups gain massive influence and success **b**.

Furthermore, the system of federalism in the USA creates numerous 'pressure points' where pressure groups can campaign and lobby. They can campaign at local, state and national level, which allows for a great deal of success.

Although the above suggests finance is not a major player in the US pressure group system, pressure groups often hire professional lobbyists to lobby the government on behalf of their cause, often ex-Congressmen. Pressure groups that can afford to 'buy' ex-Congressmen who have a lot of insight within US government often see a great amount of success **b**.

Furthermore, with the issue of success comes the issue of iron triangles. Iron triangles are the relationship between the interest group, a congressional committee and a government department, an example being the military iron triangle or the agricultural one. These relationships are regarded as being undemocratic, as deals are made without taking into account the interests of society at large. These 'special relationships' are not open to all pressure groups, yet interests such as healthcare and tobacco enjoy such privileges. Gaining such an access point to the government **b** is extremely advantageous to pressure groups and inevitably leads to a great deal of success.

Another factor that can cause US pressure groups a great deal of success is events. After the Columbine shootings and Clinton's attempts at having a 'cooling off' period before a gun purchase in 1993, the National Rifle Association (NRA) faced trouble. Yet they campaigned that if guns were widely available someone could have shot the killers before mass murder took place. This event, although damaging to the NRA, in fact publicised their cause.

Finally with regard to the NRA, their success lies in the fact that guns are seen as part of the constitutional right in the USA to bear arms. With the constitution behind them, no politician dares challenge them **b**.

In conclusion, there are various factors that lead to disproportionate levels of success within US pressure groups.

e **b** This answer, although quite focused and containing some relevant AO2 analysis, such as the success of the NRA and iron triangles, suffers because many arguments are not developed enough for high AO2 marks: for example, the relationships between access points and success or between publicity and success are not clearly expressed, lowering potential AO2 and AO3 marks, and are not consistently backed up with supporting evidence and examples, such as how and why professional lobbyists can lead to success or how 'events' can lead to success. There is knowledge of PACs but little analysis of their impact on 'success'. There are some contradictions and some lack of logic in the answer regarding the role of finance in pressure group success, as well as some vague and over-generalised assertions, such as **a** that campaigning at different levels or 'hotly debated' issues or media attention leads to success. The conclusion is also brief. Overall this leads to a C rather than a B grade, with more marks being given for AO1 than for AO2 or AO3.

Knowledge check answers

1 As well as federal elections there are also elections at state (and local) levels of government. This, coupled with the separation of executive and legislative powers, leads to elections for both the executive and legislative branches of both layers of government, creating a long and complex electoral process that may lead to democratic overload and voter fatigue.

2 Caucus selection is mainly used in more rural states and is dominated by the base of politically active, registered party supporters likely to be more liberal in the Democratic Party and more conservative in the Republican Party. This means that candidates will run somewhat ideologically different campaigns in these states, to the left in the Democrat caucuses and the right in the Republican. The Iowa caucus in particular, therefore, is not always a reliable predictor of who is going to win.

3 The 'invisible primary' is the period when candidates declare their intention to run, visiting early-voting states usually a year before the first primary vote. They jostle for position as the front runner, to gain momentum through media attention, increasing name and face recognition and campaign donations. Candidates fade or drop out if they cannot achieve these. The 'winner' of the invisible primary is not guaranteed to win the nomination, so it is not always 'significant' in predicting the winner.

4 The long and extremely gruelling nature of the primaries can be likened to Darwin's 'survival of the fittest'. Only the candidates suited to what will be the gruelling nature of running the executive branch will survive the tests that primaries force upon candidates to prove that they are capable of winning the presidency. Weaker candidates will drop out or be defeated along the way because they do not have what it takes to win.

5 Primaries are divisive contests where the party candidates attack each other to win voter support, as the attacks on Obama by Hillary Clinton showed in 2008, so the party can appear disunited by the time of the convention. Voters dislike divided parties, shown by the Republican Party's 1992 defeat after a bruising primary contest between G. Bush and Pat Buchanon. So in order to present a 'united front' at the convention, 'political wounds' have to be healed through speeches and visible support.

6 The Democratic Party Hunt Commission introduced super-delegates in 1984 to bring an element of 'peer review' into the nomination process. Approximately 20% of convention delegates are not committed by primary or caucus vote. They are the party's hierarchy and elected officials who can vote for whichever candidate they think would be best for the party. They have never influenced the selection because the winner has always had enough delegates to win outright, but they could be significant in a very close race.

7 Presidential campaigns are run by paid, professional political consultants who determine the strategy and tactics of the campaign. Candidates rely on such advisers to help them win, such as Clinton's reliance on James Carville, G. W. Bush's on Karl Rove and Obama's on David Axelrod. There are also pollsters, media advisers and spin doctors who make up the campaign team of 'hired guns', which is one reason why so much money is needed for campaigns.

8 Modern electoral campaigns focus on 'marketing' the candidates themselves and their media image rather than the party or policies, leading to highly personalised campaigns and specialist advisers working for candidates rather than parties. This is criticised as focusing on more trivial 'style' factors such as likeability and how candidates look rather than serious policy issues of substance.

9 Candidates try to gain as much 'free media' as possible through photo-opportunities or newsworthy events, to get their campaigns into the broadcast media and news, increasing name and face recognition without using precious campaign finance to pay for publicity. This is contrasted with advertising that must be paid for in expensive television slots. Most campaign money is spent on these paid commercials, especially on prime-time television in key states.

10 After FECA, most presidential candidates accepted federal funding for their campaigns. However, with escalating campaign costs, wealthy candidates who have amassed large war chests are now more likely to reject such funding and the spending limits that come with it. Bush and Kerry rejected federal funding in 2004, as did Obama in 2008 despite originally saying that he would accept it. As a result he had a huge financial advantage over McCain, who accepted $84 million of federal funds. Obama's decision resulted from a spectacularly successful fund-raising campaign through the internet and social media.

11 The 1st Amendment guarantees freedom of speech, which extends, according to the Supreme Court, to spending in support of, or opposing, candidates through 'independent expenditures' (so-called 'political speech'). So it is impossible to restrict campaign finance when individuals or organisations can legally donate unlimited sums of money to independent groups such as the 527s and Super PACs to use for 'issue advocacy' or to fund their own campaigns.

12 This rare event occurs because the Electoral College has a winner-takes-all system in 48 out of 50 states. This means a candidate can win a state by a small margin of votes but then receive all that state's EC votes, as Bush did in Florida in 2000 with only 547 votes more than Gore, but gaining all the state's 27 EC votes. Votes for a candidate can also pile up in safe states but are only adding to the popular vote total. So the popular vote can be high but just not won in places where it counts.

13 'Faithless' electors who fail to vote for the candidate who won their state's popular vote have occurred in six elections since 1960, with nothing to prevent this constitutionally. They have little significance because individual 'rogue' electors have never had any impact on the outcome of a presidential election, usually just making some political point of their own, but they could be highly significant in a tied or very close EC vote.

14 The mechanism of the EC arises directly from its origins within a federal state with jealously guarded states' rights. It is the 50 states that elect the president, based on their state representation in Congress (plus DC), and this suits both small and large states for different reasons, so they would be unlikely to vote to change this system through a constitutional amendment.

15 Direct democracy mechanisms are simply an 'add on' to the normal decision-making process in the legislatures of the states that use them. The majority of state decisions are made after debate and deliberation by representatives taking decisions on behalf of the people whom they were elected to represent. Referendums and initiatives are not replacing but supplementing this process.

16 Referendums originate from state legislatures, which may decide to consult the voters for approval or disapproval, either before or after making a decision. They are top down because they are put to the people. Initiatives originate from the people themselves attempting to put a proposition onto the ballot paper through signature petitions in their states and so are described as bottom up (although the process may have been 'hijacked' by special interests).

17 Direct democracy devices are triggered by gathering petition signatures from registered voters in order to place a question on the ballot paper. Because states decide their own decision-making processes, this will vary between states. The number of signatures needed relates to the voter turnout at the last election and is usually between 5 and 15% of that voting population to prevent frivolous and frequent ballot petitions.

18 The term 'realignment' refers to fundamental changes to the electoral coalitions supporting the parties, leading to a change in party dominance because of shifts in voting behaviour, as seen during the Great Depression in the 1930s and the elections of that period. Since then there has been no sign of either a permanent Republican or Democrat majority appearing. However, the South realigned to the Republican Party in the 1960s and the 'solid' Democrat South is now a Republican stronghold.

19 The New Deal Coalition of votes that gave the Democratic Party majority party status from the 1930s to the 1960s (bar the Eisenhower presidency) broke down under the pressure of internal contradictions where the conservative, white southern voters who had supported the party since the civil war voted for the same party as the more liberal minority, blue-collar and radical intellectual voters from the northern states. The party's move to support civil rights and lifestyle changes in the 1960s led to the breakaway of the white South and some conservative blue-collar workers from this voting coalition.

20 The loss of the South and 'Reagan Democrats' led to Democrat defeats in the 1968, 1972, 1980 and 1984 elections because of the party's perceived liberalism. The Democratic Leadership Council formed in 1985 and led by southerners such as Clinton and Gore wanted to move the Democratic Party further right towards more ideologically centrist policy positions, such as ending big government liberalism, in order to win back the presidency. This was achieved when Clinton won in 1992 and 1996 helped by this party faction, regarded by some critics as 'Republican Lite'.

21 In the 1994 mid-term election the Republican Party, under the leadership of Newt Gingrich, stood under the banner of the Contract with America — in effect, a national manifesto proposing very conservative policy positions such as a balanced budget to win the House for the Republicans. This 'manifesto', part of the 'Republican Revolution', led to a clearly more ideologically conservative Republican Party under speaker Gingrich, although most of the proposals did not pass or were vetoed by Clinton.

22 Democrats favour activist, federal government intervention in the economy and greater regulation, as they believe that only the federal government can create more fair and equal conditions as seen in the New Deal and Great Society programmes, Obama's healthcare reforms and regulation of the banks. Republicans, in contrast, favour little government intervention in the free market, creating incentives for individuals to work harder and the private sector to create jobs with less regulation and smaller, more limited government, balanced budgets and states' rights.

23 Because of rising deficits, bailouts and stimulus intervention started by Bush and continued by Obama, the Tea Party movement started to press for changes to the economic direction of the country and greater fiscal conservatism. The movement has pushed the Republican Party further to the right, seen in the Tea Party candidates in the 2010 mid-terms, the influence on the 2012 primaries and the Republican agenda generally, perhaps alienating more moderate Republicans in the process.

24 In the federal USA, parties are organised at state level and operate under state law. They are de-centralised in structure with little if any control by the national party through the DNC and RNC, unlike the centralised, national UK parties. This means that there are big differences between state parties depending on the state and its characteristics. The state parties only meet every 4 years when their delegates attend the nominating conventions. Therefore, the USA is said to have a 50- or 100-party system with each party being different in the 50 states.

25 In a two-party-dominated political system, third parties' only chance of making an impact would be to have some influence on the political agenda of the time or the outcome of a single election. Most are short-lived and based around individual candidates and single issues that are often ignored by the two main parties, such as Wallace in 1968 (civil rights), Perot in 1992 and 1996 (budget deficits) and Nader in 2000 and 2004 (environmental issues). However, though votes can be gained by these third-party candidates and issues can be raised, most fail to survive and benefit simply from short-term protest votes.

26 States are described as 'red' (Republican) or 'blue' (Democrat) because of their loyalty to one or other of the parties. This is because states have very different social, ethnic, racial and demographic features within them. The red Republican states are mainly the more rural/suburban states in the South or the Midwest, such as Utah or Alabama, with a majority of Republican voters, and the blue states are the more liberal Northeast states such as Massachusetts and Vermont, socially and ethnically diverse states such as California and the more industrial states such as Illinois. Some 'swing' states, however, have a more 'purple mix' within them and are not dominated by one party.

27 Unlike the UK, which developed from a feudal system with a defined social hierarchy and where it is said that 'class is the basis of voting behaviour', the USA lacks a sense of class consciousness with over 90% of Americans defining themselves as 'middle class' through lifestyle. In the USA, other divisions such as race, ethnicity, religion and region are more significant in explaining political identity, attitudes and voting behaviour.

28 The black vote has been heavily Democrat since the 1930s and the Democratic Party therefore feels it does not have to win over this group of voters by making appeals specifically to them. The Republican Party, achieving only 5% of the black vote in 2008, knows there is little point appealing to voters whom it cannot win.

29 Hispanics are the largest growing minority in the USA and their vote is significant in many battleground states with high Electoral College votes. Largely Spanish speaking and Catholic, their vote has been 'up for grabs' in recent elections where many were energised to vote by the moral values focus of the Republicans in 2004 and the more favourable views on immigration and welfare of the Democrats in 2008. As their numbers increase, both parties will target them as a key group of voters to win over.

30 Older voters are more likely to turn out to vote in elections than younger voters, as they have a stronger partisan alignment and feel it is their democratic duty to vote. As a result their interests are more likely to be focused on by parties seeking to maximise votes, such as prescription drug benefits or healthcare and support in old age.

31 Two examples of voters with cross-cutting identifications would be: a Hispanic, Catholic, male, chief executive living in the suburbs of Chicago in Illinois; and an unmarried female, white Protestant living in a rural area in Kansas and working as a civil servant in the public sector. There are many other combinations that can illustrate the difficulties of predicting the way a person is going to vote based solely on social characteristics.

32 In the 2004 presidential election the issues that dominated the election were moral values focusing on abortion and gay marriage and also national security issues as this was the first election after 9/11 and the War on Terror. In 2008 these issues were less salient and the focus was on 'the economy, stupid' because of the recession, bank bailouts and two unpopular and costly wars.

33 The voting age population (VAP) is the term for all residents in the USA over the age of 18. The voting eligible population (VEP) excludes non-citizens living in the USA and convicted felons who lose the right to vote, sometimes permanently depending on state law; it is regarded as a more accurate measure and when used will give a higher figure for turnout at elections.

34 Voter turnout rises and falls at different elections depending on the engagement of the electorate and the successful mobilisation of the vote. The lowest turnout was in 1996 with 53% of eligible voters voting (49% of VAP) whilst the highest turnout was 64% of eligible voters in 2008. Fluctuations relate to the different candidates and voters' perceptions of them and the dominating issues that differ at each election as well as how close the election is seen to be.

35 Countervailing groups (or lobbies) are those which oppose or counteract one another on a specific issue, providing some degree at least of pressure group balance. Examples are the 'pro-choice' (NARAL Pro-Choice America or Planned Parenthood) and 'pro-life' groups (National Right to life) on the issue of abortion, and pro- (National Rifle Association) and anti- (Handgun Control Inc) gun control groups.

36 These are groups organised around, and advocating for, a single issue as opposed to multiple issues. Examples are groups such as the gun lobby, the NRA, groups focused on protecting the environment such as the Sierra Club and the Jewish lobby AIPAC, focused on pro-Israel policy. Single-issue lobbies can be fanatical and intense in their focus and activities, such as 'pro-life' groups on the issue of abortion.

37 Groups supporting liberal, progressive or minority causes are more likely to support the Democrats, such as the NAACP representing African-Americans and the AFL/CIO representing organised labour. Groups supporting business or religion are more likely to support the Republicans, such as the US Chamber of Commerce, the National Association of Manufacturers (NAM) or Focus on the Family (pro-traditional values) as well as the gun lobby, the NRA.

38 In contrast to the UK, the Supreme Court's power of constitutional interpretation and judicial review makes it an important access point for pressure groups that wish to influence its decisions in areas connected to their interest or cause. As a result, groups like the NAACP and ACLU submit Amicus Curiae briefs, sponsor litigation in test cases and try and influence the nomination and confirmation processes for Supreme Court justices when a vacancy arises, to try and influence the selection of either judicially 'liberal' or 'conservative' justices.

39 Pressure groups try and influence the election of politicians sympathetic to their interest or cause, or alternatively try and negatively target those who oppose them for defeat. They can make hard money contributions to campaigns through PACs, or 'spend on behalf of' using issue advocacy, which since the Citizens United case has been unrestricted, and has led to the rise of Super PACs. They do this because they would like to gain access to politicians if they win or to remove politicians who may oppose their aims and objectives.

40 The revolving door spins or recycles politicians and officials out of elected or appointed office and into lucrative positions in lobbying organisations usually in the K Street Corridor, after a 2-year 'cooling off' period brought about by the Honest Leadership and Open Government Act of 2007. It can be argued that this is an abuse of public service and potentially corrupt as they are exploiting insider contacts and expertise gained when in office for monetary gain. Three out of four oil and gas lobbyists previously worked in the federal government.

41 PACs are criticised because their 'hard money' campaign contributions to electoral candidates, which are often 'bundled', lead to a perception that politicians can be 'bought' and that you have to 'pay to play'. It is feared that PAC contributions may influence the voting intentions of elected politicians, who are elected to represent their constituents not pressure groups with PACs. However, there is little evidence of any clear link between PAC contributions and roll call votes in Congress.

Page numbers in **bold** refer to **key term definitions**

A

abstention 38–40
access points 43, 46
age 36
Asian vote 35

B

balanced ticket **12**
ballot access 31
battleground states *see* swing states
'big tent' internal coalitions 23, 27, 31
Bipartisan Campaign Reform Act (BCRA) 16–17
black vote 34–35
blanket vote 20, 42, 45
Blue Dog Democrats 25

C

campaign finance 15–17, 29, 44
candidate voting 37
catch-all parties 23, 31, 45
caucuses 9–10, 51–52
clientelism 44
closed primaries 10
compassionate conservatives **26**
Congress 43, 44, 46–47
congressional party committees 15
conservatism **25**
Contract with America 25, 27
core voters 33–34
cross-cutting identifications 37

D

de-alignment **38**
debates 14–15
democratic overload 9, **39**

Democratic Party 23–25, 27, 29, 30, 34–35, 36
differential abstention **40**
direct action **45**
direct democracy 20–21, 51–56
duopoly 19, 30, 31

E

economic pressure groups 41
Electoral College 18–19, 31, 39, 52–56
electoral process 9–22, 51–56
elite theory **41**
ethnicity 34–35
Executive Office of the President (EXOP) 43

F

FEC v *Citizens United* 17, 47
Federal Election Campaign Act (FECA) 15–16, 46
Federal Election Commission (FEC) 16, 17
federal funding 16, 29, 31
federalism 18, 28, 38
federal structure 9
financing of campaigns 15–17, 29, 44
fixed terms of office 9
free media 14
front-loading 10
fund-raising 11, 15, 17, 46

G

gender gap **36**
GOP (Grand Old Party) *see* Republican Party
grass-roots lobbying 45
grey vote 36
gridlock 38

H

'hapathy' 39
hard money **16**, 29
Hispanic vote 35
Honest Leadership and Open Government Act 2007 46
House of Representatives 19, 43
hyper-pluralism 42

I

ideological resurgence 29–30
income 34
incumbency effect 13
initiatives 20–21, 45
internal coalitions **27**, 31
invisible primaries 10, 11
iron triangle **44**
issue voting 37

J

judicial branch 43

L

legislative branch 43
liberalism **24**
lobbying **44**

M

'Main Street' wing, Republicans 26
mass mailing campaigns 45
media and election campaigns 13–15, 29, 31–32, 39
momentum **9**

N

national nominating conventions 11–12
national party committees 15
negative campaigning **14**
New Deal Coalition 23–24, **34**
New Democrats 25
New Hampshire primary 10

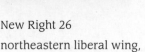
New Right 26

northeastern liberal wing, Democrats 25

O

open primaries 10

organisational resurgence 30

outsider candidates **11**

'outsider' strategies, pressure groups 44–45

P

paid media 14

partisan alignment 31, 33

partisan de-alignment 29, 37–38

partisanship 29, 33, 39, 64–65

party decline 28–30

party identification **33**, 64–65

party organisation 28

party renewal 29–30

performance voting 37–38

permanent campaigning 9, 11, 15, 39

personalised campaigns 14, 29

pluralism **41**

political action committees (PACs) 15, 29, 46–47

political parties 23–33, 57–63

popular vote 10, 18–19

presidential campaign 12–13

pressure groups 20, 21, 29, 31, 41–47, 69–74

primaries 10–11, 29, 31, 51–52

professional lobbyists 44

public campaigns 45

public interest lobbies 42

R

race 34–35

realignment 23, 25

recall elections 21

recency factors 37–38

referendums 20–21

region 36–37

religion 35–36

religious right 26, **27**

Republican Party 25–27, 29, 34, 35

'revolving door' 44

Rockefeller Republicans 26

S

Senate 19, 43

separation of powers 9, 28, 38

single-issue groups 29, 31, 42, 46

soft money **16**

southern conservative wing, Democrats 24–25

split-ticket voting **38**, 65–68

super-delegates 12, 30

Super PACs 15, 17, 47

Super Tuesday 10

Supreme Court 17, 43

swing states **13**, 18–19

'swing' voters **37**

T

Tea Party movement 27, 29

television advertising 14

third parties 31–32, 59–63

Third Way politics 25

triangulation 25

two-party system 30–32, 59–63

U

UK electoral processes 22

UK parties 32

UK pressure groups 47

UK voting behaviour 40

V

vice-president 12, 19

voter apathy 39

voter choice 34–37

voter fatigue 39

voter registration 38–39

voting behaviour 33–40, 64–68

W

'Wall Street' wing, Republicans 26

wasted votes 30

weak parties 28, 57

winner-takes-all system 10, 18, 19, 30

women voters 36